An Introduction to the Shoshoni Language

An Introduction to the Shoshoni Language

Dammen D<u>a</u>igwape

Drusilla Gould and
Christopher Loether

The University of Utah Press
Salt Lake City

21 20 19 18 17
5 4 3 2

The excerpt on page 5 by Chevalier de la Varendrye is from Ann Blegen,
"Journal of the Voyage made by Chevalier de la Varendrye with one of
his Brothers in Search of the Western Sea." In *Oregon Historical Quarterly*
26(2)1925:118. Quoted by Mark Q. Sutton, "Warfare and Expansion: An
Ethnohistoric perspective on Numic Spread," *Journal of California and*
Great Basin Anthropology 8(1)1986:71.

Library of Congress Cataloging-in-Publication Data

Gould, Drusilla, 1951–
    An introduction of the Shoshoni language : dammen daigwape /
Drusilla Gould and Christopher Loether.
        p. cm.
Includes bibiographical references and index.
    ISBN 0-87480-729-8 (hardcover : alk. paper) —
ISBN 978-0-87480-730-1 (pbk. : alk. paper)
    1. Shoshoni language—Phonology. 2. Shoshoni language—Grammar.
3. Shoshoni language—Dialects—Idaho—Fort Hall Indian reservation.
I. Loether, Christopher, 1958– II. title.
    PM2321 .G68 2002
    497'.45—dc21

                                                2002010188

Contents

Chapter 3. **Masen newe du hagai' nanihade?**

Chapter 6. **Himb<u>ai</u>'gandei' ennem bungu ba'i?**

Chapter 7. Maitengate hagai' neesungaahka?

Chapter 8. Beaichehkuse, hinna enne hanni'yu?

Chapter 9. **Hagapunde sikihyunde?**

Acknowledgments

We wish to gratefully acknowledge the Social Science/Humanities Research Council at Idaho State University for its financial support that made recording the lessons possible. We want to thank Jason Johnson and Kristin Fletcher for allowing us to use some of their writings in Shoshoni. We also would like to thank Michael D. Jensen for his excellent editing job, and Debra Castle and Kristin Fletcher for all of their hard work with the Shoshoni-English and English-Shoshoni glossaries in the original edition of this book, and all of the other students we have had in our Shoshoni classes over the years at Idaho State University for thier helpful comments and suggestions on how to improve the text.

Finally, we would like to dedicate this book to all speakers of the Shoshoni language—past, present, and future.

How to Use this Book

As an introduction to the Shoshoni language, this book focuses on the dialects spoken on and around the Fort Hall Indian Reservation in southeastern Idaho, but other dialects are also discussed throughout the course. The purpose of the book is to give the student, or reader, a solid foundation in the Shoshoni language. This book alone cannot teach someone to speak, read, and write Shoshoni. The student will need to seek out Shoshoni-speaking people to help in learning the language. This step is especially important to the student of Shoshoni, since there is not a large amount of printed material in the language. Shoshoni has always been, and still is, primarily a spoken language. Besides the writing system used in this book, there are two other writing systems in common use throughout the Shoshoni-speaking world, one of which, the most widely published, is introduced in this course.

The product of many years of teaching the Shoshoni language to both Shoshoni and non-Shoshoni people, on and off the reservation, this course was developed and tested for a decade in Shoshoni language classes at Idaho State University, Pocatello, Idaho, which is eight miles south of the Fort Hall Indian Reservation. The material in this book takes two to three semesters to cover, depending on the pace of the classes.

Drusilla Gould, a native speaker of the Lemhi and Fort Washakie dialects of Shoshoni and an enrolled member of the Shoshone-Bannock tribes, has been involved in teaching, preserving, and promoting her native language for over two decades. Christopher Loether, an anthropological linguist and director of the American Indian Studies Program in the Department of Anthropology at Idaho State University, has been working with Ms. Gould on the Shoshoni language since 1989, and on Numic languages in general since 1979.

The first chapter deals with the pronunciation of the language and how to write it. It is important that students spend an adequate amount of time practicing and mastering the sounds of Shoshoni. A set of tapes is available to accompany the text of this book. Students are encouraged to listen to the tapes as often as possible. It is also important to repeat the sounds, words, and sentences aloud in the pauses provided on the tapes. Arrows in the left margins of the text indicate taped material. At the end of Chapter 1 is a list of all the grammatical terms used throughout the course and their meanings.

Chapters 2 through 8 follow a general pattern. Each one begins with a list of objectives followed by two dialogs. The dialogs are based on real life scenarios and are designed to give students practice and confidence in dealing with similar situations in the language. Each dialog is provided with a vocabulary, an English translation, and a literal translation. The literal translation shows the differences between the English and Shoshoni ways of expressing the same idea. The student is encouraged first to review the new vocabulary and then learn the dialog by heart. One method of practicing the dialog is to repeat it aloud, altering the content by substituting words within the dialog. The dialogs are followed by a Language and Culture section, which contains important cultural information relating to Shoshoni society and language use. It is our firm belief that one must be familiar with cultural norms in order to learn and use a language successfully, especially a nonwritten language such as Shoshoni. The Grammar section of each chapter introduces important concepts and rules associated with using the Shoshoni language correctly. Finally, Chapters 2 through 8 end with drills to give students further practice in the new grammatical constructions introduced and vocabulary lists. A student is encouraged to master completely all the information in a lesson before moving on.

Chapter 9 contains a number of short readings in Shoshoni. They are designed to give students practice in writing Shoshoni and to increase their vocabulary. This chapter also provides suggestions for further study of the language as well as a list of works on the Shoshoni and their culture and language.

A Shoshoni–English Glossary, followed by an English–Shoshoni Glossary, contains all the words used in the course.

Introduction

The Shoshoni Language

The Shoshoni language is spoken by approximately 5000 people living across Nevada, Idaho, Utah, California, and Wyoming. The 1990 U.S. Census counted 2,284 Shoshoni speakers and ranked the Shoshoni language 18th in the number of speakers of American Indian languages (U.S. Census Bureau, Washington, D.C.). These figures are not accurate because only 12 percent of the population in any one area were questioned concerning language use.

The first contact Shoshoni speakers had with Europeans and Euro-Americans was in the eighteenth century. At that time Indian languages were considered barbaric and inferior to European languages. Over the next century many Indian people were taught in schools run by the U.S. Bureau of Indian Affairs that their native languages were not to be passed on to the next generation, and some individuals were punished for speaking their native language among themselves. As a result, this negative attitude toward Native American languages has now caused a decrease in the number of children learning their native language. Consequently, most of the Native American languages still spoken in the United States are in danger of dying out within the next 100 years.

Origins of the Shoshoni Language

Linguists are able to reconstruct earlier forms of languages, even though there are no written records of these languages. Reconstructed languages are known as "protolanguages." The protolanguage of English is Proto-Germanic, the mother language from which all the modern Germanic languages have descended, such as English, German, Dutch, Swedish, etc.

The Shoshoni people do not have a written history, so their history exists in oral stories and archaeological remains. The protolanguage

3

from which Shoshoni descended is known as "Proto-Numic." It is the
mother language of all the modern Numic languages, such as Shoshoni,
Bannock, Southern Paiute, Ute, Mono, etc.

Reconstruction of Proto-Numic produces close approximations of the
words that were used by the speakers of this extinct language. Analysis
of the reconstructed words can yield important information concerning
the physical environment of the early speakers, their material culture,
their social and political structures, their religion and world view. Proto-
Numic speakers practiced a hunter-gatherer lifestyle, were seminomadic,
and politically and socially organized into bands (groups of people who
live together and cooperate economically with one another, but are not
necessarily related to one another). After the first Europeans arrived in
the Great Basin (Nevada and Utah), the Numic-speaking peoples continued to live in bands, a basic structure that had not changed for millennia.

The bands were guided by a "headman" (known as a **daigwahni'** in
Shoshoni, from the verb root **daigwa-** "to speak"). He was usually a
gifted speaker and his duties were prescribed by tradition. Dissatisfaction with a headman usually led to choosing a new leader. A headman
used only the power of persuasion during group decisions, and his most
important group decisions concerned when the band was to break camp
and what food resource to exploit next.

Based on a careful analysis of the words in Proto-Numic for plants,
animals, waterfowl, fish, insects, and physical features of the environment, Dr. Katherine Fowler of the University of Nevada-Reno has identified a "linguistic homeland" of the Proto-Numic people, that is, where
the speakers of Proto-Numic were living before the protolanguage broke
up into the various dialects that became the modern Numic languages,
such as Shoshoni ("Some Ecological Clues to Proto-Numic Homelands,"
pp. 105–21 in *Great Basin Cultural Ecology: A Symposium*, edited by Don
Fowler, University of Nevada, Desert Research Institute Publications in
the Social Sciences no. 8, 1972). She believes this area to be along the eastern slopes of the southern Sierra Nevada mountains in what is today
eastern California. This particular area contained the right combination of
plants, animals, etc., represented in the reconstructed words from Proto-
Numic at the same time period (approximately 1000–2000 years ago).

The Names "Shoshoni" and "Snake" Indians

"Shoshoni" (also spelled "Shoshone" with no change in pronunciation
or meaning) comes from the Shoshoni word **sosoni'**, which is the plural
form of **sonipe**, a type of high-growing grass. Several tribes on the Plains

referred to the Shoshoni as the "Grass House People," which probably refers to the conically shaped houses made of native grasses (**sosoni'**) used by the Great Basin Indians. The name "Shoshone" was first recorded in 1805 by Meriwether Lewis after he encountered a group of "Sosonees or Snake Indians" among the Crow and noted it in his diary.

The earliest written record about the Shoshoni referred to them as the "Snake Indians." The Snake River of southern Idaho, previously known as the South Fork of the Columbia River, is named after these same "Snake Indians." In 1742 the Frenchman Pierre Gaultier de Varennes (also known by his title "Chevalier de la Varendrye") wrote:

> These Snake Indians are considered very brave. They are not satisfied in a campaign to destroy a village, according to the custom of all other Indians. They continue their warfare from spring to autumn, they are very numerous, and woe to those whom they meet on their way! . . . They are friendly to no tribe. We are told that in 1741 they had entirely destroyed seventeen villages, had killed all the old men and old women, and made slaves of the young women and had traded them at the seacoast for horses and merchandise.

The Shoshoni were called the "Snake People" by some of the Plains Indians. The origin of the term "Snake People" is based on the sign Shoshoni people used for themselves in Indian sign language. The hand motion made for the sign represents a snake to most signers, but among the Shoshoni it referred to the salmon, an unknown fish on the Great Plains. Today many Shoshoni people have adopted the term **sosoni'** to refer to groups of Shoshoni other than themselves. The more common term used by Shoshoni people is simply **newe** "people."

Origin of the Shoshoni People

The prehistory of the Shoshoni people—how their ancestors, known as the "Numa" by archaeologists and prehistorians, were able to occupy portions of the Great Basin and continguous areas (Nevada, Utah, Idaho, and Wyoming)—is a highly debated topic. The origin of the Numa is believed to be the southwestern corner of the Great Basin. By 1500 the Shoshoni had crossed the Rocky Mountains and begun their expansion and control over the northwestern Plains. By 1700 a group of Shoshoni had moved into the southern Plains and eventually developed their own identity as the Comanche. The current location of the Eastern Shoshoni in central Wyoming is the result of a period of intense warfare from 1780 to 1825 against the Blackfeet, Crow, and Assiniboine.

Currently the Shoshoni are widely spread across the western United States. Anthropologists divide them into three groups based on where they live: the Western Shoshoni (in Nevada and western Utah), the Northern Shoshoni (in Idaho and northern Utah), and the Eastern Shoshoni (in Wyoming). The Eastern Shoshoni were the only bands of Shoshoni speakers who completely adopted a Great Plains way of life, involving changes in their economic life, their social relations among themselves and with other tribes, and their religious ideology and ceremonialism.

History of the Fort Hall Reservation

The Fort Hall Indian Reservation, home to the Shoshone-Bannock tribes, is located in southeastern Idaho. It currently comprises 544,000 acres and is home to 5,114 persons (according to the 1990 census), of whom 3,035 (or 59.3 percent) claim American Indian descent. As of 1991, there were 3,528 enrolled members of the Shoshone-Bannock tribes (data from the Business Council, Shoshone-Bannock Tribes of the Fort Hall Reservation). The earliest non-Indians in eastern Idaho was a group of fur trappers led by Andrew Henry, who in 1810 wintered on Henry's Fork (which is named after him) in the upper Snake River Valley after being driven out of the Missouri River Forks area north of there by the Blackfoot Indians.

From 1818 until 1832, there were regular fur-trapping expeditions, known as the "Snake expeditions," into Shoshone-Bannock country. One American trapper, Nathaniel J. Wyeth, traveled through southeastern Idaho in 1832 and set up a trading post on the Snake River bottoms in 1834. Wyeth named Fort Hall after the rich Easterner who put up most of the money to finance his venture. Within two years, Wyeth's Fort Hall was bankrupt and was eventually sold to the British fur-trading enterprise, the Hudson's Bay Company, in 1838. The Hudson's Bay Company ran the trading post until it closed in 1852.

The opening of the Oregon Trail in 1840 brought many new people through Shoshone-Bannock country, which led to increasing tensions between the Shoshone-Bannock and the westward migrating pioneers. This situation culminated in the Shoshoni War of 1860–1863, after which the United States government began an active program of signing treaties with all the various Shoshoni bands throughout Nevada, Utah, Idaho, and Wyoming.

The first treaty signed between the Shoshone-Bannock and the United States government was the Treaty of Soda Springs, Idaho Territory, signed on October 14, 1863, with Tahgee, Tasokwauberaht (also known as "Le Grand Coquin" by the French-speaking fur trappers), and Matigund representing the Shoshone-Bannock. Chief Tendoy of the Lemhi Valley gave his approval to the treaty, even though he was unable to attend the actual signing ceremony because of bad weather. This treaty, however, was never ratified by the United States Congress.

Another treaty, the Treaty of Fort Bridger (1868), established the Wind River (Wyoming) and Fort Hall (Idaho) Reservations. President Andrew Johnson signed the treaty on February 24, 1869, and the Fort Hall Reservation officially opened in April 1869. The opening of the reservation began a period of ethnic cleansing and hardship for the Shoshone-Bannock unlike anything they had ever experienced before. They were forcibly removed from their homes and sent to the reservation. On the reservation they found little food, no opportunities, and very little hope for the future.

The Bannock War of 1878 was a direct result of the dissatisfaction with the unlivable conditions suffered by the Shoshoni on the reservation. A group of Bannock warriors under the leadership of Chief Buffalo Horn rebelled against the United States authorities and tried to rally other Indians in Nevada, Idaho, and Oregon. Chief Buffalo Horn and his warriors were finally caught four months later in September 1878.

The town of Pocatello, located eight miles south of the Fort Hall Reservation, was founded in 1890, after the Shoshone-Bannock agreed in 1888 to cede 1600 acres to the government. The town was originally a switching station between the Utah and Northern Railroad (which ran from Salt Lake City, Utah, to Montana) and the Oregon Short Line. The Shoshone-Bannock ceded another 418,500 acres as the town continued to grow. Congress ratified this land cession in 1900, and President Roosevelt opened it for white settlement on May 7, 1902. Another 28,000 acres were ceded in 1924 in order to allow construction of the American Falls Reservoir.

The United States government eventually discontinued the reservation system that had been set up and passed the Dawes Severalty Act of 1887, which gave individual Indian men their own land. In accordance with this act, the Fort Hall Reservation was surveyed in 1892, and between 1911 and 1913 there were 1,863 allotments, mostly consisting of 160 acres apiece, assigned to individual Shoshone-Bannock men. This situation was reversed in 1934, following the passage of the Indian Reorganization Act, which allowed the reorganization of the tribal governance system. After the adoption of a formal constitution and bylaws, the Shoshone-Bannock tribes of the Fort Hall Reservation became a legal and sovereign entity on April 17, 1937.

1

Shoshoni Orthography and Pronunciation

The Shoshoni Writing System

All languages are unique, finite systems: they have different inventories of sounds, different ways of combining those sounds into words, and different ways of putting those words into coherent speech in order to meet all the demands of communication within the particular society in which they are used. Because of these basic differences between languages, the system of writing (or orthography) used for one language is not appropriate for writing another language. There are various ways of representing sounds graphically, but one of the most widely used is the Roman alphabet, so called because it was the ancient Romans who first designed the letters that we use today in writing English (and many of the other European languages). The Romans had adapted their letters from the Greek alphabet (through the Etruscans) in order to represent more accurately the sound differences between ancient Greek and ancient Latin.

Although there are many languages that use the Roman alphabet, most of the letters in these modern languages do not reflect their exact sound value in classical Latin, nor would one expect them to since all languages have a different inventory of sounds. Nor would one expect all languages that use the Roman alphabet to have the same sounds represented by the same letters. In English the letter "z" represents one sound, while in German "z" represents the sound [ts] as in "cats," and in some Spanish dialects it represents the sound [th] as in "think."

There is a strong tendency among people literate in English to write other languages that do not have a written tradition using what is known as an "English-based orthography." This writing system gives letters of the Roman alphabet the same values as in written English, but it is a system that must be avoided when writing Shoshoni since many of the sounds in Shoshoni are absent in English, plus the English writing system is very inconsistent. It accurately reflects, however, the history of the English language. Our writing system was fixed relatively early: in the late 1400s, when the pronunciation of the language was noticeably different than it is today. Letters that were pronounced then (such as the word final "e" in "wine") but no longer pronounced today are still reflected in the spelling of a word. Also, there have been many loanwords, especially from French, incorporated into English that do not reflect an English pronunciation because they have retained a non-English spelling. To truly understand English spelling conventions one must know how the language was pronounced five hundred years ago, with all the sound changes that have occurred between then and now, as well as the rules governing medieval French pronunciation and spelling.

The Shoshoni orthography used in this course is based on several earlier ones. Many of the orthographies have not been popular among Shoshoni speakers, and therefore have not been widely adopted and used, because they were too phonemic (i.e., they reflected an abstract level of the language and did not look the way they are pronounced, at least not to the literate English speaker's eye). The orthography used here is more phonetic (i.e., it reflects more closely the actual pronunciation of the words). Unlike English, each letter or combination of letters (known as a "digraph") has one and only one pronunciation, so that you should be able to pronounce accurately all new words that you encounter. Any discrepancies in spelling and pronunciation are due to dialectical differences, discussed further in Chapter 2.

Remember to be consistent when using the orthography: always use the same letter or combination of letters to represent the same sound. When you come across a new word, try writing it out in the Shoshoni orthography. If you are unsure about how to write something, ask your teacher to show you. The more you write in Shoshoni, the easier it will become.

Shoshoni Sounds and Pronunciation

VOWELS

start of
Tape 1-a

Shoshoni has the following vowels: **a, e, i, o, u,** and **ai**. The vowels can occur short or long. When they are long, they are written doubled (**aa, ee, ii, oo, uu, aaii**) and their pronunciation is generally held twice as long as for a short vowel.

Shoshoni vowels are pronounced only roughly like the following English vowels:

a   as in "hot"
e   as in "put"
i   as in "beet"
o   as in "coat"
u   as in "who"
ai as in "get"

Remember that the English sounds are only close approximations and in order to properly pronounce the Shoshoni vowels you must hear them pronounced by a native speaker of the language. If you do not have access to a native speaker, then you must listen often to the tapes that accompany these lessons. Listen closely to the following examples of each of the vowels:

a: **ada'** ("mother's brother," "male cousin," "sister's son/daughter" [male speech]); **ha** (QUESTION PARTICLE) (OBJECT CASE MARKER)
aa: **baa'** ("water"); **haa'** ("yes")
e: **ege-** ("new"); **enne** ("you" [singular])
ee: **neesungaahka** ("it feels"); **sadee'** ("dog")
i: **iki** ("right here"); **nammi'** ("younger sister")
ii: **siipungu** ("sheep"); **biidennu** ("has/have arrived")
o: **dogo'** ("maternal grandfather," "grandchild(ren) by one's daughter" [male speech]); **mo'** ("hand")
oo: **gotoo'** ("fire"); **gotoonoo'** ("stove")
u: **u** ("him," "her," "it," "them"); **yuhu** ("fat")
uu: **yuuta'** ("Ute Indian"); **duu-daiboo'** ("black person," "African-American")
ai: **baide'** ("daughter"); **gai'** ("no")

DIPHTHONGS

Diphthongs are more than one vowel sound that are pronounced as one. Shoshoni has a number of diphthongs that generally sound like a blending of the two different vowel sounds. They are pronounced only roughly as follows:

ai   as "igh" in English "high"
ea   as "u" in "put" followed by "a" in "about"
eai as "u" in "put" followed by "ay" in "hay"
ei   as "u" in "put" followed by "ee" in "bee"

ia as "ia" in "Maria"
oi as "oy" in "boy"
ua as "oo" in "too" followed by "a" in "about"
ui as "ewy" in "chewy"

Listen to how the following examples are pronounced by a native speaker:

ai: daiboo' ("white man," "Euro-American"); hainji ("male friend")
ea: dease ("also," "too"); mea' ("moon")
eai: be<u>ai</u>chehku ("morning")
ei: dei' ("female friend" [female speech])
ia: bia' ("mother"); mia' ("let's go")
oi: newezoika'i ("Nez Perce Indian")
ua: dua' ("son")
ui: bui ("eye")

VOICELESS VOWELS

Shoshoni has a group of vowels that do not occur in English. They are voiceless (or whispered) vowels. Voiceless vowels occur most commonly in rapid, connected speech. If the final vowel of a word is preceded by one of the following consonants, ch, k, p, s, sh, t, or ts, it will normally be voiceless. This is sometimes also true of vowels that occur between any of the seven consonants within a word. In the following examples the voiceless vowels are written in capital letters, although normally they are written like any other vowel:

sogopE "land"
masE "this, that" [contrastive]
natEsu' "medicine"
<u>ai</u>kwEhibitE "purple"

CONSONANTS

Shoshoni has the following consonants: b, ch, d, dz, f, g, h, hk, hn, hs, ht, hw, hy, j, k, m, mm, n, ng, nn, p, s, sh, t, ts, w, y, z, zh, and '. Be aware that most of these letters stand for sounds that are not found in English. The letters ch, h, hw (same as English "wh"), j, m, n, ng, s, sh, ts, and z have approximately the same values in both English and Shoshoni, while all the other letters represent sounds substantially different from their English sounds.

ch as in "church"
h   as in "hat"

hw   as "wh" in "which"
j   as in "jam"
m   as in "mom"
n   as in "now"
ng as in "finger" and not as in "singer"
s   as in "soon"
sh as in "ship"
ts as in "cats"
z   as in "zoo"

The consonants **b, d,** and **g** have two different pronunciations. Which of the two pronunciations they take is based on where they occur within the word. They are pronounced with what is known as a "hard pronunciation" when they occur at the beginning of a word and with a "soft pronunciation" when they occur between two vowels within a word. All the hard sounds are stops; they are made by stopping the flow of air through the mouth and nose. The soft sounds are all fricatives; they are made by allowing air to flow through a restricted cavity in the mouth or nose.

When **b, d,** or **g** occur at the beginning of a word, they have a hard pronunciation and are pronounced as follows:

b   as the "p" in "spy"
d   as the "t" in "stay"
g   as the "k" in "sky"

When the hard sounds occur between vowels within a word, they are written as **p, t,** and **k** but are still pronounced as follows:

p   as the "p" in "spy" but held slightly longer
t   as the "t" in "stay" but held slightly longer
k   as the "k" in "sky" but held slightly longer

Here are some examples:

iki "right here"
ape' "father"
gotoo- "to make fire"

When **b, d,** and **g** occur in the middle of a word between two vowels, they have a soft pronunciation and are pronounced as follows:

b   as the "v" in "have" but without the lips touching the teeth
d   as the "tt" in "better" when pronounced fast
g   as the sound made when gargling, but softer

When a hard sound occurs within a word between two vowels, there are two different ways of writing this: as either **p, t,** and **k** as shown above, or **b, d,** and **g** when the hard sound is the result of two different words being combined into a single word:

> **duu-daiboo'** or **duutaiboo'** "African-American"
> **Soo-gahni** or **Sookahni** "Blackfoot, Idaho" (literally, "many houses")
> **sii-bungu** or **siipungu** "sheep"

Following are examples of the consonants. Note that the consonants **ch, f, hk, hn, hs, ht, hw, hy, j, k, mm, ng, nn, p, sh, t, z,** and **zh** cannot be used at the beginning of words. Notice also that the words below are pronounced in a "pausal" or "citation" form, which can be very different from the more fluent form of the word used in connected speech:

b: **baa'** ("water"); **bazi'** ("older sister"); **babi'** ("older brother"); **sohoo'bi** ("tree"); **saa'bai** ("in there")

ch: **huchuu'** ("bird"); **beaichehku** ("morning"); **guchu** ("cow")

d: **deheya'** ("deer"); **dosabite** ("white"); **ada'** ("mother's brother," "male cousin," "sister's son/daughter" [male speech]); **doyadaiboo'** ("Hispanic," "Mexican"); **gedii'** ("cat")

dz as "dz" in "adze": **Dzoon** ("John")

f as the sound made when blowing out a candle: **naafaite** ("six"); **dakáweife'nni** ("it's snowing")

g: **gaa'** ("rat"); **gapai** ("bed"); **sogope** ("land"); **daga'** ("male friend" [male speech, archaic]); **basigoo'** ("Indian potato," "camas root")

h: **haa'** ("yes"); **haga'** ("where"); **ohapite** ("yellow")

j: **hainji** ("friend" [male speech])

k: **iki** ("right here"); **duka** ("under"); **duku** ("meat," "mountain sheep"); **maiku** ("okay," "alright")

hk as an audible "h" before the "k": **beaichehku** ("morning"); **beaichehkuse** ("in the morning")

m: **mu'bii** ("car"); **muu'bi** ("nose"); **mia'** ("let's go")

mm as "m" in "ham" but held twice as long: **damme** ("we" [pl/inclusive]); **dommo** ("winter"); **memme** ("you" [pl])

n: **naniha** ("name"); **nawa'aipe'** ("wife," "brother's wife" [male speech]); **banabui** ("window")

nn as "n" in "on" but held twice as long: **enne** ("you" [singular]); **bannaite'** ("Bannock Indian"); **hi'nna** ("what")

hn as an audible "h" before the "n": **gahni** ("house"); **guhnaiki** ("to run" [toward the speaker]) ng: **bungu** ("horse"); **ba͟ingwi** ("fish"); **wenangwa** ("in front of")

p: **siipungu** ("sheep"); **tso'ape** ("ghost"); **ape'** ("father")

s: **sosoni'** ("Shoshoni Indian")

hs as an audible "h" before the "s": **buhihseagu** ("sprouting")

sh: **ishe** ("this" [close enough to touch] [contrastive]);
    ga͟ishe ("not yet")

t: **nazatewa'** ("door"); **yuuta'** ("Ute Indian")

ht as an audible "h" before the "t" or as "th" in "both":
    himba͟igandengahtu ("for how much" [money])

ts: **tsaa'** ("good"); **tsadamani** ("Chinese person"); **tsiina'** ("potato")

w   generally as in "wind," although when between two vowels it
    can take on a strong nasal quality (this is caused by letting air
    escape through the nose): **wongoo'bi** ("pine tree"); **wenangwa**
    ("in front of"); **waapi** ("Utah juniper"); **dowoahka** ("it's
    cloudy"); **nee'we** ("person," "Indian," "Shoshoni Indian");
    dawi' ("younger brother")

hw: **nehwe** ("we" [dual/exclusive]); **dahwe** ("we [dual/inclusive])

y   generally as in "you," although when between two vowels it can
    take on a strong nasal quality: **yamba** ("wild carrots," "yampa
    root"); **yuhutegumahanipe** ("fry bread"); **guyungwi'yaa'**
    ("turkey"); **ga͟iyu'** ("late")

hy as an audible "h" before the "y," similar to "hu" in "huge":
    wihyu ("then," "and then," "but"); **dapa͟ihyaa'** ("sock[s]")

z: **bazi'** ("older sister"); **nazatewa'** ("door")

zh as "s" in "vision": **gizhaa'** ("not good"); **da͟i'zhi** ("sister's hus-
    band" [male speech])

'   is known as the "glottal stop." It is pronounced by cutting off
    the flow of air in your throat as in "uh oh": **bia'ape'** ("father's
    older brother"); **ba'i** ("to have"); **a'aa'** ("Crow Indian");
    da'oo' ("dried," "powdered meat"); **gadenoo'** ("chair");
    bia' ("mother"); **haa'** ("yes")'

FINAL FEATURES

Shoshoni also has a series of silent consonants at the ends of words
known as "final features." They occur only when followed by a word
that begins with a specific sound. There are three final features in
Shoshoni, represented by the following symbols at the end of a word:
-N, -', and **-H**.

The first final feature (**-N**) is known as the "nasalizing" final feature.

It is pronounced as an **n, ng,** or **m** depending on what sound the following word begins with. Here are the rules:

> a) if the following word begins in **d, n,** or **ts,** it is pronounced **n;**
> b) If the following word begins in **g,** it is pronounced **ng;**
> c) if the following word begins in **b** or **m,** it is pronounced **m;**
> d) if the following word begins with any other consonant, it is silent.

Here are some examples of the different forms **-N** can take, using the word **nemmeN** "our" [pl/exclusive]:

> **nemme ape'** ("our father")
> **nemmen daga'** ("our friend" [male speech])
> **nemmen nammi'** ("our younger sister")
> **nemmen tsiina'** ("our potato")
> **nemmen genu'** ("our paternal grandfather")
> **nemmem bia'** ("our mother")
> **nemmem mu'bii** ("our car")

The second final feature (**-"**) is known as the "geminating" or "hardening" feature. This feature causes the initial sound of the word that follows, if beginning in **b, d,** or **g,** to remain hard. When two words are combined, and the second word begins in either **b, d,** or **g,** a hyphen is inserted between the two words. For example, when the prefix **duu"-** "black" is added to **daiboo'** "white man," "Euro-American," the new word is written **duu-daiboo'** (with a hyphen) to indicate that the second **d** is also a "hard" sound. Another example is the word **sii-bungu** "sheep," which is the result of **sii"-** "urine" + **bungu** "horse."

The third final feature (**-H**) is known as the "pre-aspirating" final feature. This feature is the least common of the three. In theory it adds an "h" sound to the sound of the following word, but in reality almost all the pre-aspirated forms of consonants change their sound significantly. The only four sounds that are not significantly altered are **-H + n → hn, -H + s → hs, -H + w→ hw, -H + y → hy.** For example, **buhihseagu** "sprouting" is the combination of **buhiH-** "green" + **seagu** "growing." Here are the other combination of sounds with the pre-aspirating final feature: **-H + b → f; -H + d → ht; -H + g → hk; -H + m → hw; -H + ts → sh.**

If a word is combined with another word, and the first word does not end in a final feature, initial **b, d, g, n,** and **ts** in the following word will take the "soft" sound. For example, when you combine **doya-** "mountain" and **daiboo'** "white man," "Euro-American," you get **doyadaiboo'** "Hispanic," "Mexican," where the first **d** has the "hard" sound and the second **d** has the "soft" sound. Here are further examples illustrating this point, where each is pronounced as if a single word:

> **ne dekákuandu'i** is pronounced as [**nedekákuandu'i**]
> **ne dease** is pronounced as [**nédease**]
> **newe tsoiga'i** is pronounced as [**néwezoiga'i**]
> **gai ne** is pronounced as [**gáiye**]

Note that, although nasalizing final feature (**-N**) is the most common of the final features, the other final features are still an important part of the Shoshoni sound system and are extremely important when combining elements, either prefixes or words, into compounds. More will be covered about the final features in future lessons.

STRESS ACCENT

Shoshoni is regularly accented on the first syllable of a word. When the stress falls on another syllable, it is indicated by an acute accent over the stressed vowel (**á, é, í, ó, ú, ái**). For example, the word **dekákuandu'i** "will go to eat" is stressed on the second syllable and therefore contains an accented vowel, whereas the related word **dekape** "food" is accented on the first syllable and therefore has no accented vowels.

MINIMAL PAIRS

Minimal pairs are pairs of words that are nearly identical, except for one or more slight differences in sound. You must learn to hear the subtle differences between these pairs, and be sure to pronounce them differently. Here is a list of some common miminal pairs in Shoshoni:

deheya' ("deer")	**dehe'ya** ("horse")
mu'bii ("car")	**muu'bi** ("nose")
daga' ("friend")	**da'ga** ("only," "just")
no'yo ("egg")	**noo'yo** ("testicle")

Words of Advice

It is important to listen to the tape (or a native speaker) and try pronouncing the various sounds and words as much as possible until you feel comfortable and natural in producing all the different sounds. Sometimes it may take as many as fifty to seventy times before you can pronounce a new sound correctly. Do not become discouraged; just keep at it.

Glossary of Grammatical Terms

Adjective – describes a noun or pronoun, such as "red" in English.

Adverb – describes a verb, adjective, or other adverb. Adverbs of time describe "when" (such as "today"), adverbs of place describe "where" (such as "here"), and adverbs of manner describe "how" (such as "quickly").

Aspect – describes how an action happened. Aspect is usually shown by special suffixes added to the verb stem.

Auxiliary verb – a verb which is added to another verb.

Case – shows the grammatical relations among words in a clause or a sentence. The three cases in Shoshoni are the subject case, the object case, and the possessive case.

Code-switching – refers to the use of more than one dialect or language in the same sentence or in a longer discourse.

Completive tense – indicates that the action of the verb has been completed, usually for a while.

Conjunction – is a word that connects other words or clauses (such as "and" or "but" in English).

Continuative aspect – indicates that the action of the verb is ongoing, but only lasts for a short period of time.

Coordination – refers to how words and clauses are connected to one another. The connecting words themselves are known as conjunctions.

Customary-habitual aspect – indicates that the action of the verb is done on a regular basis for a significant stretch of time.

Demonstrative pronoun – is a "pointing" word. In English we have two, "this" and "that," along with their plural forms, "these" and "those."

Dependent clause – is a clause that cannot stand alone. Dependent clauses, which are also known as relative clauses, are connected to a main clause, which is known as an independent clause. In the previous sentence, "which are also known as relatives clauses" is itself a dependent or relative clause. Dependent clauses in English often start with "that," "which," or "who."

Dual number – refers to exactly two of something.

Durative aspect – indicates the action of the verb lasted for a length of time, emphasizing the duration of the action.

Expective tense – indicates that the speaker expects the action of the verb to occur in the future, but is not sure.

Final features – are silent consonants or consonantal processes at the end of Shoshoni words. There are three final features in Shoshoni: pre-nasalization, pre-aspiration, and gemination. The final features are sounded only when the first sound of the following word triggers their pronunciation.

First person – refers to the speaker, either "I" or "we."

Future tense – indicates that the action of the verb will occur in the future.

Gemination – is the doubling (or "hardening") of a consonant. Germinated consonants are usually pronounced twice as long as single consonants.

Gerund – refers to verbs used as nouns. In English, the gerund "singing" is used as both a verb ("I am singing") and a noun ("your singing sucks").

Imperative – is the command form of a verb, used to tell someone to do or not to do something.

Indefinite pronoun – is a pronoun that refers to a nonspecific person or object, such as "someone" or "something" in English.

Independent clause – is a clause that contains a main verb and can stand on its own.

Infinitive – is a verb form that does not indicate person or tense. In English, infinitives are formed by adding "to" to the verb, as in "to eat" or "to read."

Instrumental prefix – is a prefix added onto a verb stem to indicate how the action of the verb is done.

Intransitive verb – is a verb which does not take an object.

Iterative aspect – indicates the action of the verb was repeated quickly.

Liaison – refers to the process by which two or more words are run together and pronounced as if they were a single word. The final features are pronounced when words are run together in speech.

Nominalization – is the process whereby a verb is turned into a noun. In Shoshoni this is accomplished by adding particular suffixes to the verb stem.

Nominalized verb – is a verb used as a noun.

Nominalizing suffix – is a suffix added to a verb stem to make it into a noun.

Noun – names a place, person, thing, or abstract idea.

Number – refers to how many of an object. In Shoshoni there are three numbers: singular, dual, and plural.

Object case – indicates that the word (either a noun or pronoun) is the receiver of the action of the verb. Object case in Shoshoni is formed by the addition of a suffix to the noun.

Orthography – refers to the writing system for a language.

Past tense – indicates the action of the verb occurred sometime in the past in comparison with the present moment.

Possessive case – indicates that the word owns, or possesses, or somehow is connected closely to the following word. In English we indicate the possessive case by adding the suffix "-'s." Shoshoni also adds suffixes to the noun to indicate possessive case.

Postposition – is a word which shows a relationship between two or more nouns or pronouns. In English these words are known as "prepositions" because they come before the word they describe ("<u>on</u> the table"). In Shoshoni they are known as postpositions because they come after the word they describe (literally, "the table <u>on</u>").

Postpositional adjunct – is a suffix added to postpositions to give more grammatical information about the word(s) that the postposition describes.

Participial suffix – is a suffix added to a verb to change it into a participle, which is a verb form that can be used either as an adjective or a noun.

Plural number – in Shoshoni refers to three or more of something.

Pre-aspiration – refers to one of the final features, in which an *h* sound is inserted before the following consonant. In reality, this process often changes the consonant itself.

Prefinal verbal suffix – is a suffix added to a verb stem, but which cannot be the final suffix on a verb and must be followed by a tense/aspect suffix.

Prefix – is something added onto the beginning of a word.

Pre-nasalization – refers to one of the final features, in which an *n* is inserted before the following consonant.

Present tense – indicates the action of the verb is occurring at the time of speaking.

Progressive aspect – indicates that the action of the verb is ongoing, and will last for a long time.

Pronoun – is a word that stands in for a noun, such as "he," "this," or "something" in English.

Quantifiers – are words that indicate or ask about quantity, such as "much" and "how much?"

Relative clause – (see *Dependent clause*)

Repetitive aspect - shows the action of the verb was repeated slowly.

Resultative aspect – indicates that the action of the verb is the result of some prior action and that the action of the verb is still ongoing or regularly occurs over a period of time.

Second person – refers to the listener(s), "you."

Singular number – refers to one of something.

Subject case – indicates that the word is the agent or initiator of the action of the verb.

Subordinating verbal suffix – is a suffix added to a verb to indicate that the verb is part of a dependent clause.

Suffix – is something added to the end of a word.

Tense – refers to the time when the action of the verb occurred. In English there are three tenses: past tense, present tense, and future tense.

Third person – refers to the person(s) spoken about, "he, "she," "it," and "they."

Transitive verb – is a verb that takes an object (i.e., the action of the verb effects someone or something).

Unspecified object prefix – is added to the verb stem to indicate there is an object, but it is something nonspecific, such as "something" or "someone" in English.

Verb – is a word which shows some kind of action.

Verb stem – is the base form (or root) of the verb, without any additional prefixes or suffixes added.

Voiceless vowel – is a vowel that is whispered and therefore barely audible if at all.

wh- questions – are questions that cannot be answered with either "yes" or "no," and involve what are known as the "wh" words in English (where, when, why, who, what, and how).

2

Tsaangu be<u>a</u>ichehku
("Good morning")

- Greetings and Introductions
- Tribal and Ethnic Affiliations

Vocabulary for Dialog 1

tsaangu be<u>a</u>ichehku good morning
haa' yes
hagapundu (to) where?
enne you [singular]
    e'nne (PAUSAL FORM)
mi'a- to go, walk
    mi'a'yu am/is/are walking
    mi'aa'yu (PAUSAL FORM)
    -'yu (PROGRESSIVE ASPECT) [verbal suff]
gahni house
gahtu to [+ name of place or location] [postpos]
    gaahtu (PAUSAL FORM)
wihyu then, and then; but; how about; what about
ne I
deka- to eat
    dekákuandu'i is/are going to go eat
    -kuaN- (movement away from the speaker) [N class]
    -kuandu'i will go (away from speaker) to [+ verb]
    -du'i (FUTURE TENSE) [verbal suff]
m<u>ai</u>ku okay, alright
binnagwaseN later [N class]
eN (e, en, em) you [singular, object case] (modern) [N class]
emmi you [singular, object case] (traditional)
    e'mmi (PAUSAL FORM)

bui- to see
> **buinuhi** will see, is/are going to see
> **-nuhi** (EXPECTIVE ASPECT) [verbal suff]

Dialog 1

Mary and Sue are two students at Idaho State University. They run into each other walking from class.
> Mary: **Tsaangu beaichehku.**
> Sue: **Haa'.**
> Mary: **Hagapundu ennem mi'a'yu?**
> Sue: **Gahni gahtu. Enne wihyu?**
> Mary: **Ne dekákuandu'i.**
> Sue: **Maiku. Binnagwasen ne em buinuhi.**
> Mary: **Maiku.**

ENGLISH TRANSLATION:
> Mary: Good morning.
> Sue: Yes (it is a good morning).
> Mary: Where are you going?
> Sue: Home. How about you?
> Mary: I am going to eat.
> Sue: Okay. See you later.
> Mary: Bye.

LITERAL TRANSLATION:
> M: Good morning.
> S: Yes.
> M: To=where you go-(progressive)?
> S: House to. You then?
> M: I eat-go-will.
> S: Okay. Later I you see-expect.
> M: Okay.

Vocabulary for Dialog 2

> **tsaangu yeitatabai'yi** good afternoon (used to address two people)
> **tsaan dai neesungaahka** everything is fine (everything about us, including the listener, is fine)
> > **tsaan dai yeesungaahka** (FLUENT SPEECH FORM)
> **isheN** this/this one (close enough to touch) [CONTRASTIVE/PRESENTATIVE] (refer to Chapter 3, Dialog 2) [N class]

hagadeN who? [N class]
    hagaadeN (PAUSAL FORM)
ma'ai with [+ noun/pronoun] [postpos]
    em ma'ai with you (singular)
hainji (-ha) male friend [male speech]
Dzoon John
neaN (nean, neam) my/mine [emphatic] [N class]
naniha (nanihai) name
haganai' (from) where? (referring to a generic location)
bide- to arrive
    bidennu has/have arrived, has/have come
    biidennu (PAUSAL FORM)
    -nnu (COMPLETIVE TENSE) [verbal suff]
naite from [+ name of place] [postpos]
bannaite' (-a) Bannock Indian
sosoni' (-a) Shoshoni Indian
deaseN also, too [N class]
benneN self (here: myself) [N class]

Dialog 2

John, Bob, and Wayne are walking around the Idaho State University campus. Bob and Wayne are meeting each other for the first time.
    Wayne: **Tsaangu yeitatabai'yi.**
    Bob: **Haa'. Tsaan dai neesungaahka.**
    Wayne: **Ishe hagade em ma'ai?**
    Bob: **Ishen nea hainji Dzoon.**

Wayne and John shake hands. Wayne nods to John and says:
    Wayne: **Nean naniha Wayne. Haganai' ennem bidennu?**
    John: **Ne Fort Hall naite. Ne bannaite'.**
    Wayne: **Ne benne sosoni', Wyoming naite.**
    Bob: **Ne dease sosoni'. Ne benne Fort Hall naite.**

ENGLISH TRANSLATION:
    Wayne: Good afternoon.
    Bob: Yes (it is a good afternoon). Everything's fine.
    Wayne: Who is this with you?
    Bob: This is my friend John.

Wayne and John shake hands. Wayne nods to John and says:
    Wayne: My name is Wayne. Where are you from?
    John: I am from Fort Hall. I am Bannock.

Wayne: As for myself, I am a Shoshoni from Wyoming.
Bob: I am also Shoshoni. But I am from Fort Hall.

LITERAL TRANSLATION:

W: Good afternoon.
B: Yes. Good to=us(inclusive) it=feels-(resultative)
W: This who you with?
B: This my friend John.

Wayne and John shake hands. Wayne nods to John and says:

W: My name Wayne. Where-from you arrive-(completive)?
J: I Fort Hall from arrive-(completive). I Bannock.
W: I self Shoshoni, Wyoming from.
B: I also Shoshoni. I self Fort Hall from.

Language and Culture

GREETINGS

There are no words in Shoshoni that directly correspond to "Hi" or "Hello." Greetings usually concern questions about someone's immediate actions. For example:

Hagapundu ennem mi'a'yu? Where are you [sing] going?
Hinna enne hanni'yu? What are you [sing] doing?

There are equivalent greetings in Shoshoni to "Good morning," "Good afternoon," and "Good evening." Notice that there are two forms for "Good afternoon." One is the "dual" form and is used when addressing just two people. The other form is used in all other situations, whether addressing one person or more than two.

tsaangu be_ai_chehku good morning
tsaangu yeitatab_ai_'yi good afternoon [dual]
tsaangu yeitab_ai_'yi good afternoon (one, three, or more persons)
tsaangu yeyeika good evening

There is no Shoshoni equivalent to the English phrase "How do you do?"

GREETINGS ETIQUETTE

It is not necessary in Shoshoni to repeat the greetings "Good morning," "Good afternoon," or "Good evening." It is not considered impolite to simply answer these greetings by saying **haa'**. This means that you have acknowledged the speaker's greeting. The word **maiku** also shows agreement and can be translated as "Okay" or "Alright."

Shoshoni people customarily shake hands with each other when they meet. When introduced to another person, Shoshoni people usually give a slight nod of their heads to acknowledge the other person. They also shake hands as a way of saying "Thank you" in certain situations, such as during public gatherings, giveaways, powwows, and before leaving another person's home. Shoshoni people will often hug someone with whom they are on intimate terms, such as a close relative or friend, when they first meet and again before parting.

MALE AND FEMALE SPEECH

There are a number of differences between the way Shoshoni males and Shoshoni females speak. Sometimes they use different words to refer to the same object. For example, women say **nado'aigahni** for "toilet," "bathroom" while men generally use the word **gwida-gahni**.

Another example is the English word "friend." A male refers to his male friends as **hainji**. A more traditional word used by some males is **daga'**. A female refers to her female friends as **dei'**. A male refers to his girlfriend as **dehainji**.

Sometimes Shoshoni people use different words to refer to the same idea depending on whether they are speaking to a male or female. For example, females tend to use the word **mi'a-** "to go," "walk" in reference to themselves or other females, while males generally use the word **boyokami'a-** "to go," "walk" (literally, "to trot") when speaking about themselves or other males. Following are three different ways of saying the sentence, "Where are you [sing] going?"

Hagapundu ennem mi'a'yu? (female to female)
Hagapundu ennem boyokami'a? (male to male)
Hagapundu enne? (male to female or female to male)

There are also a number of kinship terms which are used exclusively by one sex or the other. Words used only by males are identified [male speech] and words used only by females are identified [female speech] in the vocabularies and in the glossaries at the end of the book.

INTONATION

Shoshoni has a unique intonation. It is important to imitate the intonation of native speakers. Do not imitate English intonation patterns. For example, the tone of a Shoshoni speaker's voice goes down at the end of a question, whereas, in English, questions usually end in a rising tone.

LIAISON

The French term "liaison" refers to a process where two or more words are run together. Liaison can effect the pronunciation of one or more of the words in a phrase so they sound as if they are all one word. Liaison is a common process in Shoshoni. As a beginner, you should try to speak in blocks of words run together, as native speakers do.

SPELLING AND DIALECTS

There are many dialects of Shoshoni. It is natural for native Shoshoni speakers to pronounce some of the words or phrases in this book differently. If family members or friends say words differently, then spell the words to reflect the way the words are pronounced. Learn to use the writing system consistently. Consult your Shoshoni instructor or the Shoshoni Language Homepage (<http://www.isu.edu/~loetchri>) about any questions concerning the spelling of a particular word. The following are some examples of dialectal variations:

 beaichehku or **baichu** "morning"
 maiku or **suniha** "okay, alright"
 gande or **ba'i** "to have"
 bozhee'nna or **biaguchu** or **neweguchu** "buffalo"

PAUSAL AND FLUENT SPEECH FORMS

In all languages, words are pronouced differently when spoken in isolation than when they are used in regular speech. Words said carefully in isolation are known as "pausal" forms. When people speak their language at normal speed this is known as "fluent speech."

The differences between the pausal and fluent forms of Shoshoni words may strike the English speaker as enormous, but actually they are no greater than differences in English words. For example, many English speakers commonly say "whutcha" for "what do you" or "gonna" for "going to." The process in English involves shortening the number of syllables and simplifying the words by dropping some (most often consonantal) sounds in the fluent forms.

Shoshoni utilizes a process foreign to English: devoicing vowels. This means that in the fluent forms of words a number of vowels may be-

come devoiced or whispered. This often obscures the surrounding consonants causing the word to sound significantly shortened, but to a
Shoshoni speaker's ear those sounds are still heard. In many pausal
forms of words, if the vowel of the penultimate (second-to-last) syllable
is a short vowel, it is lengthened to a long vowel and followed by a glottal stop. For example, **sohobi** "tree" becomes **sohoo'bi** in its pausal
form. Another very common process is the insertion of a glottal stop before a doubled **m** or **n** in the penultimate syllable in the pausal form. For
example, **enne** becomes **e'nne** in its pausal form. Pausal forms will be
identified as such in the Vocabularies.

Pay attention to any differences you notice between pausal and fluent forms of words, and try to imitate these differences in your own
speech. This way you will sound more fluent yourself to Shoshoni ears.

Grammar

NUMBER

Shoshoni has three categories of grammatical number: singular [sing],
dual [dual], and plural [pl]. The singular is used for a single being or
thing. The dual is used to refer to exactly two of anything, while the
plural is used to refer to three or more. Nouns, pronouns, verbs, and adjectives all show grammatical number in Shoshoni.

NOUNS

Nouns name people, places, things, and abstract concepts.
Shoshoni nouns show no grammatical gender. There is no distinction between masculine and feminine nouns, nor are there words corresponding to English "he," "she," and "it." Instead, Shoshoni speakers use
demonstrative pronouns ("this," "that," "these," and "those") in their
place. Additionally, Shoshoni has neither a definite article ("the") nor an
indefinite article ("a" or "an"). Again, Shoshoni uses the demonstrative
pronouns in place of the definite article, and the word "one" for the indefinite article.

Shoshoni nouns are normally cited in the dictionary in their "subject
case" forms, the form used when they are the grammatical subject of a
sentence. In this book the noun will always appear in its subject case form.

Shoshoni nouns have two types of endings. The first of these endings
is known as the "object case" suffix and is added directly onto the
subject case form of the noun. This suffix must be added to all nouns

when they are the object of a verb, that is, when they are acted upon through the action of the verb. The object case suffixes for all nouns appear in parentheses in the Vocabularies and in the Glossaries. The second type is known as the "possessive case" suffix, and shows possession between one noun and another. The possessive case suffixes will not be indicated in the Vocabularies and Glossaries, since they are predictable from the object case suffixes. Both the object case and possessive case suffixes are covered in Chapter 4.

FIRST AND SECOND PERSON SUBJECT CASE PRONOUNS

Pronouns are words that "stand in" for nouns. First person pronouns are used by the speaker to refer to her- or himself, such as "I" and "we." Second person pronouns are used by the speaker to refer to the listener(s), "you." Shoshoni does not have third person subject pronouns, which correspond to "he," "she," "it," and "they." Instead, Shoshoni uses demonstrative pronouns. Demonstrative pronouns are covered in Chapter 3. The following illustrates these differences in Shoshoni subject case pronouns "I" and "we":

	Singular	Dual	Plural
	I	we	we
First person	**ne**	**nehwe** [exclusive]	**nemme** [exclusive]
		dahwe [inclusive]	**damme** [inclusive]
	you	you	you
Second person	**enne**	**mehwe**	**memme**

Notice that in Shoshoni there are two different forms for "we" depending on whether the speaker is including the listener or not. The "inclusive" form includes the listener(s) and the "exclusive" form does not. Below are sentences illustrating the use of all the different subject case pronouns:

Ne sosoni' I am Shoshoni
Nehwe sosoni' We [dual, exclusive] are Shoshoni (the listener is not included as being Shoshoni)
Dahwe sosoni' We [dual, inclusive] are Shoshoni (you and I)
Nemme sosoni' We all [pl, exclusive] are Shoshoni (but you are not)
Damme sosoni' We all [pl, inclusive] are Shoshoni (including you)
Enne sosoni' You [sing] are Shoshoni
Mehwe sosoni' You [dual] are Shoshoni
Memme sosoni' You [pl] are Shoshoni

end of
Tape 1-a

FIRST AND SECOND PERSON POSSESSIVE CASE PRONOUNS

Possessive pronouns show ownership, such as "my," "your," and "our." Possessive pronouns in Shoshoni change to indicate all three numbers: singular, dual, and plural. The first person dual and plural possessive pronouns ("our") also make the distinction between inclusive and exclusive. The following illustrates these differences in Shoshoni first and second person possesive case pronouns:

start of Tape 1-b

	Singular	Dual	Plural
First person	my	our	our
	ne	**neheN** [exclusive]	**nemmeN** [exclusive]
	neaN [emphatic]	**dahaN** [inclusive]	**dammeN** [inclusive]
Second person	your	your	your
	eN [contemporary]	**meheN**	**memmeN**
	emmeN [traditional]		

Here are examples of the possessive pronouns introduced above used with the words **ape'** "father," **daga'** "friend," and **bia'** "mother." Note the changes in the final feature **-N** due to the different sound at the beginning of each word:

ne ape' my father
nea ape' my father [emphatic]
nehe ape' our father [dual, exclusive]
daha ape' our father [dual, inclusive]
nemme ape' our father [pl, exclusive]
damme ape' our father [pl, inclusive]
emme ape' your father [sing]
mehe ape' your father [dual]
memme ape' your father [pl]
ne daga' my friend
nean daga' my friend [emphatic]
nehen daga' our friend [dual, exclusive]
dahan daga' our friend [dual, inclusive]
nemmen daga' our friend [pl, exclusive]
dammen daga' our friend [pl, inclusive]
emmen daga' your friend [sing]
mehen daga' your friend [dual]
memmen daga' your friend [pl]
ne bia' my mother
neam bia' my mother [emphatic]

nehem bia' our mother [dual, exclusive]
daham bia' our mother [dual, inclusive]
nemmem bia' our mother [plural, exclusive]
dammem bia' our mother [pl, inclusive]
emmem bia' your mother [sing]
mehem bia' your mother [dual]
memmem bia' your mother [pl]

Notice there are two forms for "my" in Shoshoni: **ne** and **neaN**. The form **ne** is the more common form. It is connected through liaison to the following word and does not take the stress accent. If the speaker pauses between **ne** and the following word, stressing **ne**, this will change the meaning of the word to "I." For example:

ne daga' [pronounced **nedága'**] my friend
ne (PAUSE) **daga'** I am a friend
ne bia' [pronounced **nebía'**] my mother
ne (PAUSE) **bia'** I am a mother
ne ape' [pronounced **ne'ápe'**] my father
ne (PAUSE) **ape'** I am a father

It is very important to note that a pause is the main way of distinguishing between **ne** "I" and **ne** "my."

The second form for "I," **neaN**, is more emphatic. This means that the pronoun stresses the fact that it belongs to the speaker and not to someone else. For example: **Ishen neam bia'** "This is MY mother" (as opposed to someone else's).

The plural subject case pronouns and the plural possessive case pronouns can sound the same. Shoshoni speakers distinguish between the two when need be by pronouncing the possessive case pronouns with a long vowel and high tone at the end of each word:

nemmeN [pronounced **nemmee'**] our [pl, exclusive]
dammeN [pronounced **dammee'**] our [pl, inclusive]
memmeN [pronounced **memmee'**] your [pl]

No words, such as adjectives, can be inserted between the possessive case pronoun and the possessed noun.

WORD ORDER

Word order in English is subject-verb-object. The subject of a sentence must come before the verb and the object must come after the verb. In

Shoshoni the normal word order is subject-object-verb. However, a speaker can also change the word order in Shoshoni without changing the meaning of the sentence. Rules concerning word order are introduced throughout the book.

POSTPOSITIONS

Prepositions are words that show a relationship in either physical or metaphorical space and time to an object, such as "in," "on," "under," or "to." Shoshoni has words with similar meanings known as "postpositions." They are referred to as postpositions because they go after (post-) rather than before (pre-) the noun. Postpositions must come after the noun or name that they relate to, even with borrowed place-names and personal names. Postpositions never come before! Four postpositions introduced in this lesson are: **gahtu** "to," **ma'ai** "with, accompanied by," **naite** "from" [+ place-name], and **nai'** "from" [+ generic location]. Here are some examples:

gahni gahtu to home, to the house
Fort Hall gahtu to Fort Hall
em ma'ai with you [sing]
Bob ma'ai with Bob
Fort Hall naite from Fort Hall
Wyoming naite from Wyoming
gahni nai' [pronounced **gahni yai'**] from home, from the house

Notice that both **naite** and **nai'** are translated "from" in English. The postposition **naite** is used after specific place-names, while **nai'** is used in all other cases. There is one exception to this rule. In conjunction with the verb **bide-** "to arrive," use the postposition **nai'** in all cases, even with specific place-names. For example, "I am from Fort Hall" is **Ne Fort Hall naite**, but "I came/arrived from Fort Hall" is **Ne Fort Hall nai' bidennu**.

Notice also that the initial "n" in both **naite** and **nai'** is pronounced as a nasalized "y" sound if the previous word does not end in a final feature.

QUESTIONS

The word for "yes" in Shoshoni is **haa'**, and the word for "no" is **gai'**. One can use **haa'** to respond to something another person says. It is a signal to the speaker that the listener agrees with the statement or simply that the listener heard what the speaker said. During traditional storytelling sessions, which only take place during winter, the audience listening to the story answers **haa'** every so often in order to let the storyteller know that they are still listening to the story. If storytellers do not hear **haa'** for awhile, they assume that their audience has fallen asleep and will break off the story until the next storytelling session.

A simple "yes" or "no" will answer some questions in Shoshoni but they cannot answer others. For example, questions in Shoshoni that ask "where?" cannot be answered with "yes" or "no." These questions are known as "WH-questions" in English, because they begin with words that start with "wh," such as "where," "who," "when," "why," and "what." Yes and no questions are discussed in Chapter 3.

The intonation pattern of the voice always goes down in a Shoshoni question. Be sure to imitate the intonation of native speakers as closely as possible. This will help you to sound more fluent in the language.

WHERE?

There are three words in Shoshoni that correspond to the English word "where?" When no movement is involved, Shoshoni uses **haga'**. **Hagapundu** is equivalent to "to where?" "From where?" can be either **haganai'** (when referring to a generic location, such as "school" or "home") or **haganaite** (when referring to a specific place-name, such as "Fort Hall").

Vocabulary for Drills

haganaite? (from) where? (referring to a place-name)
Dembimbosaage Idaho Falls, Idaho (literally, stone bridge)
Soo-gahni Blackfoot, Idaho (literally, many houses)
Bohogoi' Gibson district (One of the districts of the Fort Hall Reservation, located between the towns of Fort Hall and Blackfoot.)
Saigwi'ogwai' Bannock Creek (literally, muddy river) (The westernmost district of the Fort Hall Reservation, located along Bannock Creek between Pocatello and American Falls.) (**Saigwihunu'** is an alternative name for this area.)
Botóode Fort Hall (More common among older people who are not fluent in English.)
daiboo' (-a) white person, Euro-American, Anglo-American (literally, one who writes things down/makes marks)
yuuta' (-a) Ute Indian

doyadaiboo' (-a) Mexican, Mexican-American, Hispanic (literally, mountain white man)

sii-bungudaiboo' (-a) Basque, Basque-American (literally, sheep white man)

duu-daiboo' (-a) black person, African-American (literally, black white man)

newezoiga'i (-ha) Nez Perce Indian (literally, someone who is both culturally part Shoshoni and Yakima)
  newe tsoiga'i (PAUSAL FORM)

yamba'i (-ha) Kiowa Indian (general label for Indian people from the southern Great Plains)

baki'ehe' (-a) Blackfoot Indian

newe (newi) person, Indian, Shoshoni Indian
  nee'we (PAUSAL FORM)

Drill 1

Answer the following questions in Shoshoni:

Q1. **Enne hagai' nanihade?** What are you [sing] called?
  Ne naniha . . . My name is . . .
  Nean naniha . . . My name is . . . [emphatic]
Q2. **Haganai' ennem bidennu?** Where do you come from?
Q3. **Enne haganai'?** Where are you from (just arrived)?
Q4. **Enne haganaite?** Where are you from?
  Ne _____ naite. I'm from _____.
  A1. **Ne Dembimbosaage naite.** I'm from Idaho Falls.
  A2. **Ne Soo-gahni naite.** I'm from Blackfoot.
  A3. **Ne Bohogoi' naite.** I'm from Gibson.
  A4. **Ne Saigwi'ogwai' naite.** I'm from Bannock Creek.
  A5. **Ne Botóode naite.** I'm from Fort Hall.
Q4. **Enne wihyu, haganaite?** And where are you from?
Q5. **Enne wihyu?** What about you?

Drill 2

Answer the following question using the various ethnic and tribal affiliations listed:

Q1. **Ne sosoni', enne wihyu?** I am Shoshoni, what about you?
  Ne . . . I am . . .
  A1. **Ne bannaite'.** I am Bannock.
  A2. **Ne sosoni'.** I am Shoshoni.

A3. **Ne daiboo'**. I am Euro-American.

A4. **Ne yuuta'**. I am Ute.

A5. **Ne doyadaiboo'**. I am Mexican-American/Hispanic/Latino.

A6. **Ne sii-bungudaiboo'**. I am Basque-American.

A7. **Ne duu-daiboo'**. I am African-American.

A8. **Ne newezoiga'i**. I am Nez Perce.

A9. **Ne yamba'i**. I am Kiowa.

A10. **Ne baki'ehe'**. I am Blackfoot.

3

Masen newe du hagai' nanihade?
("What is that called in Shoshoni?")

- Yes/no questions
- Demonstrative pronouns
- Talking about relatives
- "Do you speak . . . ?"
- "I don't understand . . ."
- "What is this called in Shoshoni?"

Vocabulary for Dialog 1

Tape 1-b (cont.)

mimi'a'yu dual form of **mi'a'yu** (see Lesson 1, Dialog 1 [Chapter 2])
    mimi'aa'yu (PAUSAL FORM)
hainji (-ha) male friend [male speech]
babi' (-a) elder brother
ha (QUESTION PARTICLE) (used to ask yes/no questions)
duN in (a particular language); with, by use of [postpos] [N class]
    newe duN in (the) Indian (language)
    sosoni' duN in (the) Shoshoni (language)
daigwa- to speak
    daigwade speak/speaks
    daigwaade (PAUSAL FORM)
    -deN (CUSTOMARY-HABITUAL ASPECT) [verbal suff]
deigu' (-a) a little, a little bit
u it (OBJECT CASE)
nangasumbaaduH- to understand (by hearing) [H class]
    nangasumbaaduhka understand/understands
    -ka (RESULTATIVE ASPECT)
ne deigu'a u nangasumbaaduhka I understand it a little
nehe ma'ai with us [dual, exclusive]
mia' let's go (used only in reference to walking)
demase then

37

Dialog 1

Duffy and Jolene attend classes at Idaho State University. They happen to run into each other on campus one morning. Jolene is with her older brother Pete.

Duffy: **Tsaangu beaichehku.**
Jolene: **Haa'.**
Duffy: **Hagapundu mehwe mimi'a'yu?**
Jolene: **Nehwe dekákuandu'i.**
Duffy: **Ishe hagade e ma'ai? E hainji ha?**
Jolene: **Gai', ishen ne babi'. Ishem Pete.**
Duffy: **Pete, enne ha sosoni' dun daigwade?**
Pete: **Gai', ne deigu'a u nangasumbaaduhka.**
Jolene (to Duffy): **Enne ha nehe ma'ai?**
Duffy: **Maiku. Mia' demase.**

They all leave.

ENGLISH TRANSLATION:
Duffy: Good morning.
Jolene: Yes (it's a good morning).
Duffy: Where are you two going?
Jolene: We're going to eat.
Duffy: Who is this with you? Your friend?
Jolene: No, this is my older brother. This is Pete.
Duffy: Pete, do you speak Shoshoni?
Pete: No, but I understand a little.
Jolene (to Duffy): Do you want to join us?
Duffy: Okay! Let's go then.

They all leave.

LITERAL TRANSLATION:
D: Good morning.
J: Yes.
D: To-where you-two going-(dual)?
J: We(dual, exclusive) eat-go-will.
D: This who you with? Your friend (question particle)?
J: No, this my older-brother. This Pete.
D: Pete, you (question particle) Shoshoni in speak-(habitual)?
P: No, I little it-(object case) hear-know-(resultative).
J: You (question particle) we (dual, exclusive)-with?
D: Okay. Let's-go then.

Vocabulary for Dialog 2

hutsí (-a) paternal grandmother; grandson (by one's son) [female speech]
>**hutsí** (VOCATIVE) (form used for calling)

maseN this/that (neutral distance) [contrastive] [N class]

newe (newi) person; Indian; Shoshoni (Indian)
>**nee'we** (PAUSAL FORM)

>**newe duN** in (the) Shoshoni (language) (pronounced [**newedu**])

hagai'? how? what?

naniha- to be called, be named
>**nanihade** is called, is named (CUSTOMARY/HABITUAL ASPECT)

>**nanihaade** (PAUSAL FORM)

hagai' nanihade? what is (it) called? (pronounced [**yanihaate**] here)

nazatewa' (-a) door

mai they say, people say, it is said (QUOTATIVE PARTICLE)

madeN this/that (neutral distance) [N class]

banabui' (-a) window

ideN this (close enough to touch) [N class]

isheN this (close enough to touch) [contrastive] [N class]

gadenoo' (gadenoo'a) chair

aideN this (not close enough to touch) [N class]

ba'ande (-ba'ande) above [postpos]
>**daha-ba'ande** above us two [dual, inclusive]

>**daha"-** we [dual, inclusive]

aisheN this (not close enough to touch) [contrastive] [N class]

degupita' (-a) (electric) light

adeN that (over there) [N class]

aseN that (over there) [contrastive] [N class]

daigwape (-ha) language, speech, word(s)
>**daiboo'an daigwape (-ha)** (the) English (language)

gai not

Dialog 2

Duffy lives with her paternal grandmother on the Fort Hall Reservation. Today she is sitting home with her grandmother practicing Shoshoni.

Duffy: **Hutsí! Masen newe du hagai' nanihade?**
Grandma: **Masen nazatewa' mai nanihade.**
Duffy (pointing to the window): **Made wihyu?**

Grandma: **Banabui'**.
Duffy (touching her chair): **Ide wihyu?**
Grandma: **Ishen gadenoo'**.
Duffy (pointing to the ceiling light): **A̲ide wihyu daha-ba'ande?**
Grandma: **A̲ishen degupita'**.
Duffy (pointing to the television set): **Ade wihyu?**
Grandma: **Asen television**.
Duffy: **Television? Asen daiboo'an da̲igwape**.
Grandma: **Haa', asen ga̲i newe dun nanihade**.

ENGLISH TRANSLATION:

Duffy: Grandma! What is that called in Shoshoni?
Grandma: That is called a "door."
Duffy: (pointing to the window) What about that?
Grandma: That's a "window."
Duffy: (touching her chair) What about this?
Grandma: This is a "chair."
Duffy: (pointing to the ceiling light) What about that up there?
Grandma: That's a "light."
Duffy: (pointing to the television set) What about that over there?
Grandma: That's a television.
Duffy: Television? That's an English word.
Grandma: Yes, there's no Shoshoni word for that.

LITERAL TRANSLATION:

D: Grandma (paternal)! That Indian in how is-called-(habitual)?
G: That door they-say is-called-(habitual).
D (pointing to the window): That then?
G: Window.
D (touching her chair): This then?
G: This chair.
D (pointing to the ceiling light): This then we(dual, inclusive)-above(at rest)?
G: This light.
D (pointing to the television set): That then?
G: That television.
D: Television? That white man's word.
G: Yes, that not Indian in is-called-(habitual).

Language and Culture

MORE ON LIAISON AND FINAL FEATURES

Notice that if a word ends in a final glottal and is followed by another word, the final glottal is dropped and the word is treated as if it did not end in a final feature. The two words should be treated as a single word.

There are several phrases in this lesson affected by this process. The phrases **sosoni' duN** and **mia' demase** are pronounced as if single words ([**sósonidu**] and [**míademase**]).

Note also what happens when a word ends in the geminating final feature (-"), as in the case of **daha"-** "we" [dual, inclusive] when it is connected to the postposition **ba'ande** "above." In order to show that the "b" in **ba'ande** retains its hard sound (which is caused by the geminating feature at the end of **daha"-**) the word is connected to **daha"-** by a hyphen (-) to show that they should be treated as a single word in pronunciation. The same is true for **newezoiga'i-duN**, where the internal hyphen shows that the "d" in **duN** has retained its hard sound (written "t" when intervocalic or occurring between two vowels). This is because **newezoiga'i"** ends in the geminating final feature.

THE SHOSHONI KINSHIP SYSTEM

Many English speakers may be under the impression that most or all cultures use equivalent terms for relationships they have with those people around them, especially those related by blood, but this is simply not the case. Many cultures have systems that are very different from ours.

Kinship terms are used in reference to those people you consider to be relatives. In Shoshoni society the kinship term by which a person is referred often reveals how one acts toward him or her. If two people call each other "mother" and "daughter," they will tend to act more like a mother and daughter toward one another, even if they are not related by blood.

The Shoshoni system may seem confusing at first to Anglo-Americans, but it is really quite simple if one keeps in mind some of the main differences between the two systems:

1) Shoshoni distinguishes between relatives on the paternal or father's side, and relatives on the maternal or mother's side, when those concerned are separated by two generations.

2) In Shoshoni your father's brothers are referred to as fathers. And

your mother's sisters are referred to as mothers. Therefore, the term "uncle" can only refer to your mother's brothers (**ada'**), and the term "aunt" can only refer to your father's sisters (**baha'**).

3) Your brother's children, if you are male, are also your children. Your sister's children, if you are female, are also your children.

4) A female refers to her sister's husband as her husband. She calls him husband and treats him like a husband, and he treats her like a wife in all aspects of life except for sexual relations. In addition, a female treats the children of her sister and her brother-in-law, her nieces and nephews, as if they were her own children.

5) A male calls his brother's wife his wife. He treats her like a wife, and she is also expected to treat him like her husband in all aspects of life except for sexual relations. A male also treats the children of his brother and his sister-in-law, his nieces and nephews, as if they were his own children.

6) Shoshoni distinguishes between older and younger brothers, sisters, and paternal uncles (your dad's older and younger brothers). The following are all the Shoshoni kinship terms:

ape' father
bia' mother
dua' son
baide' daughter
genu' paternal grandfather
hutsi' paternal grandmother
dogo' maternal grandfather
gagu' maternal grandmother
babi' older brother; older male cousin
dawi' younger brother; younger male cousin
bazi' older sister; older female cousin
nammi' younger sister; younger female cousin
bia'ape' father's older brother; your uncle
dei'ape' father's younger brother; your uncle
ada' mother's brother; your uncle or your mother's male cousins
baha' father's sister; your aunt or your father's female cousins
ada' your sister's children [male speech only]
baha' your brother's children [female speech only]
nadainape' husband
nawa'aipe' wife
genu' your son's children [male speech only]
hutsi' your son's children [female speech only]
dogo' your daughter's children [male speech only]

gagu' your daughter's children [female speech only]
nawa'aipe' your brother's wife; your sister-in-law [male speech only]
dai'zhi your sister's husband; your brother-in-law [male speech only]
bahambia' your brother's wife; your sister-in-law [female speech only]
nadainape' your sister's husband; your brother-in-law [female speech only]
nagaha'ape' stepfather
nagaha-bia' stepmother
nagaha-dua' stepson
nagaha-baide' stepdaughter

Notice that **bia'** means both "mother" and "aunt" (mother's sister). "Aunt" can be translated as either **baha'** or **bia'** depending on how that person is related in Shoshoni culture.

Notice also that the following terms are reciprocal in Shoshoni: **genu', hutsi', dogo', gagu', ada'**, and **baha'**. This means that, for example, the grandfather and grandchildren call each other **genu'** (if the relationship is paternal) or **dogo'** (if the relationship is maternal). All the reciprocal terms in Shoshoni refer to relationships that are two generations apart. This includes grandparents with grandchildren and aunts and uncles with neices and nephews.

VISITING A SHOSHONI HOUSE

Rules of etiquette or polite behavior differ from culture to culture. What may seem a natural reaction to a situation in one culture may be horribly rude or insulting in another. Therefore, you should learn as many of the unwritten cultural rules as possible to avoid embarrassing yourself and hurting another person's feelings. Language fluency involves more than just knowing how to put words together into sentences.

Traditionally, a visitor took off their store-bought shoes before entering a Shoshoni house, whereas moccasins were allowed. This behavior is considered rather old-fashioned today. However, there are some older people who still follow this traditional custom and require that people remove their shoes before entering their home. Only store-bought shoes must be removed. You can wear moccasins in any Shoshoni house. Watch what other people are doing and follow their example.

It is customary for a Shoshoni host or hostess to offer guests some type of food and/or drink. However, it is not customary for a Shoshoni host or hostess to ask guests what they would like to have. Guests are expected to eat and drink whatever is served to them. Do not refuse food and drink for whatever reason—it is extremely rude. If a visitor is not hungry, it is polite to nibble at the food and drink. But be sure to try everything. Sometimes a host will cook a full meal for guests, and it is considered rude for the guests to leave the house before having something to eat, no matter how long it takes to prepare.

Unless a person is family or a close friend it is rude to look someone directly in the eyes, even when a Shoshoni person is simply talking to you. Therefore, if someone has business to discuss with Shoshoni people, it is best to talk about business while eating. Eating distracts people from looking at each other while talking. This way, Shoshoni people feel more comfortable talking to people with whom they are less familiar.

Menstruating women must be careful when visiting a Shoshoni home. In the homes of traditional people menstruating women should stand as near to the door as possible, and may be asked to leave. This is because traditional Shoshoni believe that a menstruating woman can cause men to become sick. The period of separation begins four days before a woman's menses and ends four days after. Also, menstruating women should never handle food that others will be consuming.

Sometimes guests bring a small gift to give to the host or hostess before they leave. For example, when visiting a Shoshoni person for advice or to learn about something it is considered polite to give a little gift. Three gifts that guests should not give are

1) Food. This is not considered a proper gift for a guest to give.
2) Alcoholic Beverages. These are illegal on most Indian reservations.
3) Flowers. These signify death and are only appropriate at funerals.

Grammar

INTRODUCTION TO THE SHOSHONI VERB

A verb describes an action. To eat, to sleep, to run, and to talk are all verbs, because they describe some kind of action. Verbs in English change form depending on when the action of the verb takes place. This is referred to as the "tense" of the verb. For example, in English, "-ed" added to a verb shows that the action happened in the past.

Shoshoni verbs are very different from English verbs, and there is no one-to-one correspondence between tenses in Shoshoni and English. Shoshoni verbs are generally very specific to a certain situation.

For example, there is no word in Shoshoni that corresponds to the

English words "to carry." To use a verb that means "to carry" in Shoshoni one must select a word depending on the shape and weight of the object that is carried, as well as specifying how one carries it.

Shoshoni verbs consist of a root with added prefixes and suffixes. The root is the part of the word that has the basic meaning of the verb. The root is always given first in the vocabulary sections, followed by a hyphen (-), and any other specific forms of the verb are listed indented below the root.

Prefixes are added at the beginning of the root to indicate how the action is carried out. For example, the prefix **tsi-** is added to the beginning of a verb to indicate that an action is carried out with "a long, pointed object."

Suffixes are added to the end of the root to specify the time the action takes place (tense) and the manner of the action (aspect). These endings are called the "tense/aspect suffixes." What follows are discussions of the seven so far introduced.

-'yu (PROGRESSIVE ASPECT) AND
-pe'nni/-fe'nni (CONTINUATIVE ASPECT)

The suffix **-'yu** is known as "progressive," because it is used to describe actions that are ongoing over a period of time. The suffixes **-pe'nni** and **-fe'nni** are known as "continuative," because they describe actions that are ongoing and are continually happening over and over. Although the action is ongoing, it is of shorter duration than the actions described by the suffix **-'yu.** For example, the word **deka-** means "to eat." The progressive form (**deká'yu**) refers to an action that is ongoing and lasts for a certain length of time, such as when people are eating a meal. The continuative form (**dekáfe'nni**) implies that the action may happen over and over again, but it lasts for a shorter duration than **deká'yu.** Hence, **dekáfe'nni** is used to describe eating snacks.

Depending on the final feature of the stem of a particular verb, all Shoshoni verbs can be divided into three classes.

1) Verbs that take **-pe'nni** are referred to as "geminating" or "G" class verbs. These verbs end with a geminating final feature (**-"**) and take the verbal suffix that has the hard consonant or geminated (doubled) sound.

2) Verbs that take **-fe'nni** are referred to as "aspirating" or "H" class verbs. These verbs end in the pre-aspirating final feature (**-H**) and take the softer or aspirated (breathy) sound.

3) A small number of verb roots end in the "prenasalizing" final fea-

ture (**-N**). These verbs are referred to as "nasalizing" or "N" class verbs. They behave the same as nouns that end in **-N**.

These three classes will be marked (G) for geminating, (H) for aspirating, and (N) for nasalizing.

-deN (CUSTOMARY-HABITUAL ASPECT)

The suffix **-deN** is known as the "customary-habitual aspect" because it shows that the action of the verb is customarily or habitually performed. This means that the action happens over a long period of time and is the normal state of affairs. For example:

    naniha- to be called, to be named
        nanihade is called, is named (what a person is customarily called)
        nanihaade (PAUSAL FORM)
    daigwa- to speak
        daigwade speak/speaks (what a person customarily speaks)
        daigwaade (PAUSAL FORM)

-ka (RESULTATIVE ASPECT)

The suffix **-ka** is known as the "resultative aspect" because it shows that the action of the verb is a result of a certain prior action. For example:

    nangasumbaaduhka understand/understands (by hearing)
    daigwaka speak/speaks

Notice that

    1) the form **nangasumbaaduhka** means that one understands as a result of knowing a particular language,

    2) the form **daigwaka** means that one can speak as a result of knowing a particular language,

    3) sometimes there are different forms of verbs and verbal suffixes for the negative in Shoshoni. For example, the negative form of the verb **nangasumbaaduhka** is different from the positive form: **gai nangasumbana'i'nna** "doesn't understand" (these are given in the vocabulary sections), and

    4) H-class (aspirating) verbs take **-hka**.

-du'i (FUTURE TENSE)

The suffix **-du'i** is used to show an action that will occur in the future. In the current usage, **-kuan-du'i** means "will go to do (something)." The suffix **-kuaN-** is used to indicate movement away from the speaker. Notice that it ends in a hyphen, which means another suffix must follow it in a word.

-nuhi (EXPECTIVE TENSE)

The suffix **-nuhi** is used to show that the speaker expects the action to occur sometime in the future, but is not certain that the action will actually take place. In addition, the suffix **-nuhi** is used in place of the future tense suffix (**-du'i**) when one is talking about hypothetical events in the future.

-nnu (COMPLETIVE TENSE)

The suffix **-nnu** is used to show that the action of the verb has been completed, and the effects of the action are still present. For example, the verb **bide-**, "to arrive," uses **-nnu** to indicate that the person has arrived and is still present: **bidennu** "has/have arrived."

DUAL AND PLURAL FORMS OF mi'a'yu

Shoshoni verbs do not normally change to show the grammatical category "person." This means that the verb endings do not change to show that the subject of the verb is first person (I or we), second person (you) or third person (he, she, it, or they). Here is the progressive form in the singular:

> **ne mi'a'yu** I am walking
> **enne mi'a'yu** you're walking
> **Mary mi'a'yu** Mary is walking

This verb has the same form in the plural progressive as it does in the singular:
> **nemme mi'a'yu** we (plural/exclusive) are walking
> **damme mi'a'yu** we (plural/inclusive) are walking
> **memme mi'a'yu** you all are walking
> **Dzoon-nee' mi'a'yu** John and company are walking

Notice that
　1) the verb **mi'a'yu** does not change as long as one is talking about a plural subject,

2) the suffix **-nee'**, as in **Dzoon-nee' mi'a'yu**, is actually a plural ending for nouns, but in this instance, when it is added to a proper name, it means "[so and so] and company," or "[so and so] and friends," and

3) to say the same thing about a man, the verb **boyokami'a** is used instead of **mi'a'yu**. For example, **Dzoon boyokami'a** "John is walking."

Dual forms of verbs in Shoshoni sometimes differ slightly. For example, the dual form of the verb **mi'a'yu** is **mimi'a'yu** (pronounced [**mi-wi'a'yu**]). The dual form is made by a regular process called "partial reduplication." This involves taking the first syllable of the word, such as **mi-** in the case of **mi'a'yu**, reduplicating it, and prefixing the reduplication onto the word. The dual forms of **mi'a'yu** are:

nehwe mimi'a'yu we two [exclusive] are walking
dahwe mimi'a'yu we two [inclusive] are walking
mehwe mimi'a'yu you two are walking

YES/NO QUESTIONS AND THE PARTICLE **ha**

Questions in Shoshoni that can be answered with either "yes" or "no" are marked by the question particle **ha**. A particle is a type of word that never changes its form. The question particle **ha** is usually second in the question construction. It cannot come at the beginning of a sentence, and questions in Shoshoni that cannot be answered with either "yes" or "no" do not take **ha**. For example, **Enne ha sosoni'?** "Are you Shoshoni?" or **Enne ha Dzoon?** "Are you John?"

Notice that **ha** can occur in other places within the sentence to change the emphasis. When the particle **ha** occurs after the verb it emphasizes the action of the verb. For example, the particle **ha** stresses the action of going in the first example below, and who is going in the second:

Dzoon boyokami'a ha? Has John left yet?
Dzoon ha boyokami'a? Is John going?

DEMONSTRATIVE PRONOUNS: SUBJECT CASE

Demonstrative pronouns are words that are used for pointing, such as this, that, these, and those. The Shoshoni language has more demonstrative pronouns than the English language.

Shoshoni is much more specific in indicating the distance between the speaker and the object being discussed. In Shoshoni there are six different demonstrative pronouns for the subject case depending on the distance of the object from the speaker.

Shoshoni demonstrative pronouns are made up of two parts. The first part of a demonstrative pronoun describes the distance factor and is known as the "distal prefix." The six distal prefixes are: **i-**, **ai-**, **ma-**, **o-**, **a-**, **u-**. The second part of each word is known as the "stem." The stem is the part of the word that shows the function of the demonstrative in the sentence. The following gives a list of the two stems and their distal prefixes, beginning with the demonstrative indicating the closest object, and then becoming increasingly more distant:

isheN	**ideN**	this right here (close enough to touch)
aisheN	**aideN**	this here (not close enough to touch)
maseN	**madeN**	this, that (middle distance)
oseN	**odeN**	that
aseN	**adeN**	that over there (within sight)
useN	**udeN**	that (out of sight)

Note that the final **-eN** in all of the pausal forms of these words is devoiced.

The stem, **-sheN/-seN**, is known as the "contrastive/presentative" stem. Either it is used to present something, such as "this is my friend," or it can be used to contrast something, such as "what is that called in Shoshoni?"

The stem **-deN** can also be added to the above distal prefixes. This stem is used as the more common demonstrative pronoun when introducing new information. New information is something the speaker does not assume the listener knows. Note that **-deN** is not the same as the customary-habitual verb suffix **-deN**.

The demonstrative pronouns in Shoshoni are also used for the third person pronouns he, she, it, and they. Therefore, it is important when speaking Shoshoni to be attentive to the distance of an object and whether the pronouns are being used for contrasting, presenting, or giving new information.

LIAISON AND FINAL FEATURES

When words that end in a final glottal are connected to a following word, the final glottal is dropped, and the word is treated as if it ended in the spirantizing final feature. This is part of the process of liaison (the word should be treated as if there were no final feature present at the end). For example, **sosoni' duN** is pronounced [**sósonidu**] and **mia' demase** is pronounced [**míademase**].

Words ending in the geminating final feature are indicated in the Vocabulary sections with the symbol ("). For example, when **daha"-** ("us" [dual, inclusive]) is connected to the postposition **ba'ande**, meaning "above," the word is written with a hyphen (-) in order to show that the "**b**" in **ba'ande** retains its hard sound caused by the geminating feature at the end of **daha"-**. The combination, **daha-ba'ande**, should be pronounced as if it were a single word.

Notice that the same is true for **newezoiga'i-duN** because **newezoiga'i"-** also ends in the geminating final feature. The internal hyphen (-) shows that the "**d**" in **duN** retains its hard sound.

Vocabulary for Drills

newi (object case of **newe**)
daiboo'a (object case of **daiboo'**)
bannaite'a (object case of **bannaite'**)
doyadaiboo'a (object case of **doyadaiboo'**)
sii-bungudaiboo'a (object case of **sii-bungudaiboo'**)
yuuta'a (object case of **yuuta'**)
newezoiga'iha (object case of **newezoiga'i**)
tsadamani Chinese (person), Chinese (language)
    tsadamaniha [object case]

Drill 1

Answer the following questions with **haa'** "yes," **gai'** "no," or **ne deigu'a u nangasumbaaduhka** "I understand a little." Note that only Indian languages take **duN**.

    a. **Enne ha newe dun daigwade?**
    b. **Enne ha daiboo' daigwade?**
    c. **Enne ha bannaite' dun daigwade?**
    d. **Enne ha doyadaiboo' daigwade?**
    e. **Enne ha sii-bungudaiboo' daigwade?**
    f. **Enne ha yuuta' dun daigwade?**
    g. **Enne ha newezoiga'i-dun daigwade?**
    h. **Enne ha tsadamani daigwade?**

DRILL 1, ENGLISH TRANSLATION:
    a. Do you speak Shoshoni?
    b. Do you speak English?
    c. Do you speak Bannock?

d. Do you speak Spanish?

e. Do you speak Basque?

f. Do you speak Ute?

g. Do you speak Nez Perce?

h. Do you speak Chinese?

Drill 2

Supply the questions in Drill 1 to the following Shoshoni answers:

    a. **Ne newi gai nangasumbana'i'nna.**

    b. **Ne daiboo'a gai nangasumbana'i'nna.**

    c. **Ne bannaite'a gai nangasumbana'i'nna.**

    d. **Ne doyadaiboo'a gai nangasumbana'i'nna.**

    e. **Ne sii-bungudaiboo'a gai nangasumbana'i'nna.**

    f. **Ne yuuta'a gai nangasumbana'i'nna.**

    g. **Ne newezoiga'iha gai nangasumbana'i'nna.**

    h. **Ne tsadamaniha gai nangasumbana'i'nna.**

DRILL 2, ENGLISH TRANSLATION:

    a. I don't understand Shoshoni.

    b. I don't understand English.

    c. I don't understand Bannock.

    d. I don't understand Spanish.

    e. I don't understand Basque.

    f. I don't understand Ute.

    g. I don't understand Nez Perce.

    h. I don't understand Chinese.

Drill 3

Answer the following question, naming all of the different family members:

    Q: **Ishe hagade e ma'ai?**

        A1: **Ishen ne ape'. / Ishen nea ape'.**

        A2: **Ishen ne bia' / Ishen neam bia'.**

        A3: **Ishen ne genu'. / Ishen nean genu'.**

        A4: **Ishen ne hutsi'. / Ishen nea hutsi'.**

        A5: **Ishen ne dogo'. / Ishen nean dogo'.**

        A6: **Ishen ne gagu'. / Ishen nean gagu'.**

        A7: **Ishen ne babi'. / Ishen neam babi'.**

        A8: **Ishen ne dawi'. / Ishen nean dawi'.**

A9: **Ishen ne bazi'. / Ishen neam bazi'.**

A10: **Ishen ne nammi'. / Ishen nean nammi'.**

A11: **Ishen ne dua'. / Ishen nean dua'.**

A12: **Ishen ne b<u>ai</u>de'. / Ishen nean b<u>ai</u>de'.**

A13: **Ishen ne nad<u>ai</u>nape'. / Ishen nean nad<u>ai</u>nape'.**

A14: **Ishen ne nawa'<u>ai</u>pe'. / Ishen nean nawa'<u>ai</u>pe'.**

A15: **Ishen ne hainji/dei'. / Ishen nea hainji/ nean dei'.**

DRILL 3, ENGLISH TRANSLATION:

Q: Who is this with you?

A1: This is my father.

A2: This is my mother.

A3: This is my paternal grandfather.

A4: This is my paternal grandmother.

A5: This is my maternal grandfather.

A6: This is my maternal grandmother.

A7: This is my older brother.

A8: This is my younger brother.

A9: This is my older sister.

A10: This is my younger sister.

A11: This is my son.

A12: This is my daughter.

A13: This is my husband.

A14: This is my wife.

A15: This is my (male) friend/(female) friend.

Drill 4

Practice the following questions and answers:

Q1: **Ishe ha emme ape'?**

A1: **G<u>ai</u>', ishen ne genu'. / G<u>ai</u>', ishen nean genu'.**

Q2: **Ishe ha mehe ape'?**

A2: **G<u>ai</u>', ishen nehen genu'.**

Q3: **Ishe ha memme ape'?**

A3: **G<u>ai</u>', ishen nemmen genu'.**

Q4: **Ishe ha emmem bia'?**

A4: **G<u>ai</u>', ishen ne gagu'. / G<u>ai</u>', ishen nean gagu'.**

Q5: **Ishe ha mehem bia'?**

A5: **G<u>ai</u>', ishen nehen gagu'.**

Q6: **Ishe ha memmem bia'?**

A6: **G<u>ai</u>', ishen nemmen gagu'.**

Q7: **Ishe ha emmen dawi'?**
   A7: **G<u>ai</u>', ishen ne babi'. / G<u>ai</u>', ishen neam babi'.**
Q8: **Ishe ha mehen dawi'?**
   A8: **G<u>ai</u>', ishen nehem babi'.**

end of
Tape 1-b

Q9: **Ishe ha memmen dawi'?**
   A9: **G<u>ai</u>', ishen nemmem babi'.**

DRILL 4, ENGLISH TRANSLATION:
   Q1: Is this your father?
     A1: No, this is my paternal grandfather.
   Q2: Is this your [dual] father?
     A2: No, this is our [dual, exclusive] paternal grandfather.
   Q3: Is this your [pl] father?
     A3: No, this is our [pl, exclusive] paternal grandfather.
   Q4: Is this your mother?
     A4: No, this is my maternal grandmother.
   Q5: Is this your [dual] mother?
     A5: No, this is our [dual, exclusive] maternal grandmother.
   Q6: Is this your [pl] mother?
     A6: No, this is our [pl, exclusive] maternal grandmother.
   Q7: Is this your younger brother?
     A7: No, this is my older brother.
   Q8: Is this your [dual] younger brother?
     A8: No, this is our [dual, exclusive] older brother.
   Q9: Is this your [pl] younger brother?
     A9: No, this is our [pl, exclusive] older brother.

4

Hinna enne hanni'yu?
("What are you doing?")

- "What are you doing?"
- Transitive and Intransitive Verbs
- The Verb "to Have"
- Object Case of Nouns
- Possessive Case of Nouns

Vocabulary for Dialog 1

start of
Tape 2-a

hinniN what? [subject case] [N class]
    hi'nniN (PAUSAL FORM)
ma gupa in this, in that, in it
    ma this, that, it (visible)
    gupa in/within [postpos]
tsina' (-a) potatoes
    tsiina' (PAUSAL FORM)
hinna what? [object case]
    hi'nna (PAUSAL FORM)
hanni- to do
    hanni'yu am/are/is doing (PROGRESSIVE ASPECT)
    hannii'yu (PAUSAL FORM)
yuhudegumahannipe (-ha) fry bread
domahanni"- to knead (bread dough)
    domahannipe'nni am/are/is kneading (dough)
    -pe'nni/-fe'nni (CONTINUATIVE ASPECT)
emmi you [object case] [sing]
    e'mmi (PAUSAL FORM)
dembuiH- to watch [H class]
    dembuihka am/are/is watching (RESULTATIVE ASPECT)
degwasenge' (-a) frying pan
tsayaahki- to carry (something) with both hands down low
    tsayaahki carry (it) with both hands down low (IMP)

haga'a'nna where? (in a place)
  haga'aa'nna (PAUSAL FORM)
gotoonoo' (-a) stove
duka under [postpos]
iki ma'i here it is
  iki right here
  ma'i with [postpos]
aisheN thank you [N class]
ennen tsaan denangabizhiande you are learning by listening well, you are obeying well (CUSTOMARY-HABITUAL ASPECT)
  tsaaN good [adj]; well [adv] [N class]
  denangabizhiaN- to learn by listening; obey [N class]
  denangabizhiande am/are/is learning by listening/obeying (CUSTOMARY-HABITUAL ASPECT)

Notice that one feature of Shoshoni is the presence of optional glottal stops. These are glottal stops in words that are pronounced by some speakers but not by others. For example, the word **hinna** is pronounced [hinna] by some people and [hi'nna] by others. Some people use both forms: **hinna** when the word is at the beginning of a sentence, and **hi'nna** when the word stands alone in a complete sentence, as in "what?" The optional glottal stop in this course is normally indicated as (PAUSAL FORM) following the word in the Vocabularies.

Dialog 1

Dennis is eight years old and visiting his maternal grandparents. Dennis walks into the kitchen where his grandmother is cooking.

Dennis (pointing to the big pot on the stove): **Gagú? Aishe hinni ma gupa?**
Grandma: **Tsiina'.**
Dennis: **Hinna enne hanni'yu?**
Grandma: **Ne yuhudegumahannipeha domahannipe'nni. Enne wihyu hinna hanni'yu?**
Dennis: **Ne emmi dembuihka.**
Grandma: **Degwasenge'a tsayaahki.**
Dennis: **Haga'a'nna?**
Grandma: **Gotoonoo' duka.**
Dennis (getting the frying pan from under the stove, he brings it to his grandmother): **Iki ma'i, gagu'.**
Grandma: **Aishe, ennen tsaan denangabizhiande, gagu'**

ENGLISH TRANSLATION:

Dennis (pointing to the big pot on the stove): Grandma, what's inside this?

Grandma: Potatoes.

Dennis: What are you doing?

Grandma: I'm making fry bread. And what are you doing?

Dennis: I'm watching you.

Grandma: Bring me the frying pan.

Dennis: Where is it?

Grandma: It's under the stove.

Dennis (getting the frying pan from under the stove, Dennis brings it to his grandmother): Here it is, Grandma.

Grandma: Thank you. You're a good grandson.

LITERAL TRANSLATION:

D: Grandma(maternal), this what that(visible) in?

G: Potatoes

D: What(object case) you doing?

G: I fry-bread-(object case) kneading-(continuative). You then what(object case) doing?

D: I you(object case) looking=at-(resultative).

G: Fry pan-(object case) carry.

D: Where=at?

G: Stove under.

D: Right=here with, Grandma(maternal).

G: This, you good listen-learn-(habitually) grandson.

Vocabulary for Dialog 2

guna wood
    guu'na (PAUSAL FORM)
wepagu'i- to chop
    wepagu'i'nna am/are/is chopping
    wepagu'ii'nna (PAUSAL FORM)
    -'nna (ITERATIVE ASPECT) [verbal suff]
hagani'yunde why? how come?
dommo winter (adverb); in winter; wintertime
    do'mmo (PAUSAL FORM)
daaN (alternative form of) **dahaN** [N class]
gotoo- to make a fire [intr]
    gotoope (-ha) fire [noun]

du'i will be (added to nouns to show future tense) [postpos]
mu'bii (-ha) car, automobile
mabizhiaN- to fix (something) with the hands [N class]
   mabizhiange'nna am/are/is fixing (it) with the hands
   -ge'nna (REPETITIVE ASPECT) [verbal suff]
gizhaa not good [adv]
guhnaikiN- to run (of a motor) [intr] [N class]
   guhnáikingu is running (of a motor)
   -ku (MOMENTANEOUS ASPECT)
gaisheN not yet (traditional) [N class]
   gaisheseN not yet (younger speakers)
sumbana'i'nna do/does not know (ITERATIVE ASPECT) (used only in negative)
   sumbana'ii'nna (PAUSAL FORM)
   sumbaaduhka know/knows (positive form)

Dialog 2

Dennis walks outside to where his maternal grandfather and maternal uncle are working.

   Dennis (walking up to his grandfather): **Dogó, hinna enne hanni'yu?**
   Grandpa: **Ne guna wepagu'i'nna.**
   Dennis: **Hagani'yunde?**
   Grandpa: **Dommo, daan gotoo' du'iha.**
   Dennis (walking over to his uncle): **Adá? Hinna enne hanni'yu?**
   Uncle: **Ne emmen dogo'am mu'biiha u mabizhiange'nna.**
   Dennis: **Hagani'yunde?**
   Uncle: **Gizhaa u guhnáikingu.**
   Dennis: **Hagani'yunde?**
   Uncle: **Ne gaishese u sumbana'i'nna.**

ENGLISH TRANSLATION:
   Dennis (walking up to his grandfather): Grandpa, what are you doing?
   Grandpa: I'm chopping wood.
   Dennis: Why?
   Grandpa: To burn during the winter.
   Dennis (walking over to his uncle): Uncle, what are you doing?
   Uncle: I'm fixing up grandpa's car.
   Dennis: Why?

Uncle: Because it's not running well.
Dennis: How come?
Uncle: I don't know yet.

LITERAL TRANSLATION:
    D: Grandpa(maternal), what(object case) you do-(progressive)?
    G: I wood(object case) chopping-(iterative)
    D: Why?
    G: Winter, our(inclusive/plural) fire will=be-(object case).
    D: Uncle, what(object case) you do-(progressive)
    G: I you(object case) grandpa's car-(object case) it(not visible)
      fixing=by=hand-(iterative)
    D: Why?
    U: Not=good it(not visible) run-(momentaneous).
    D: Why?
    U: I already it(not visible) not=know-(iterative).

Language and Culture

TRADITIONAL SHOSHONI COURTSHIP AND MARRIAGE

In traditional Shoshoni society prearranged marriages were normal. The parents would initiate the marriage arrangements for a young female.

An older custom of courtship involved young men playing a flute to court young women. The flute playing was a signal to the girl that the boy was interested. When she became aware that the boy was interested in her, he would then bring presents for her family. If the family did not approve of the young man, they would ignore him by turning their backs on him and not accepting the gifts. When a couple was married, they commonly lived with the bride's parents until they were financially stable enough to live by themselves.

The extended family is very common among Shoshoni households. An extended family situation usually involves three or more generations living under one roof. The advantages of an extended family are:

1) When grandparents are present in a household they can help take care of the children while the parents work.

2) An extended family situation allows older members of the community to continue fulfilling important roles and positions in Shoshoni society.

3) Elderly family members have someone to look after them in their old age.

A popular public gathering place for young people is at Shoshoni social dances. These occasions help young people in meeting one another.
The largest dance is the Annual Shoshone-Bannock Indian Festival held
during the second weekend of August at Fort Hall, Idaho. Another
Shoshoni social dance is the Courting Dance, which is held in winter at
public gatherings. In the dance, two men and two women approach each
other while dancing. If the women do not want to dance with those particular men, they turn their backs on them. Otherwise, the man puts his
right arm around the woman's waist and his left arm on her shoulder.
The woman puts her left arm on the man's waist and her right arm on
his shoulder. Married as well as single people participate in this dance.

Another Shoshoni social dance is the Owl Dance. For this dance the
women get to pick their dance partners. If a particular man does not
want to dance with a particular woman, then he must give her some
money instead. At most social dances where the men pick their partners,
it is normal for the man to give his partner some money or a gift for
dancing with him. Traditionally, men often gave their partners jewelry
and other gifts instead of money.

GIFT GIVING

Giving gifts is a very important part of Shoshoni culture. The practice of
giving gifts has become ritualized, and one can give a gift to someone
anytime. Traditionally, if a person admired another's possession, it was
considered polite to give the possession as a gift to the person. Therefore,
you must be careful not to openly admire the belongings of others, especially those of older traditional Shoshoni people. You may be put in an
awkward position of being offered things as gifts.

A giveaway is a traditional Shoshoni way of honoring someone.
Giveaways are held to honor someone's birthday or someone who has
achieved his or her goal, such as high school or college graduation. The
occasion generally includes a dinner and dancing.

The grandparents of the person being honored sponsor the giveaway. If the grandparents are not present or unable to be the sponsors,
then the parents or other close relatives can sponsor it. Putting on a giveaway can be very expensive. The sponsors supply the food, the music
for dancing, and numerous gifts of different values to be given away to
the guests. The person being honored does not receive any gifts.

During the giveaway the gifts are displayed in a central location.
Usually the sponsoring family calls guests to come forward and receive
their gifts. Guests are announced by their proper names, or by groups,

such as elders, visitors, singers, royalty, etc. The guests that receive the more expensive gifts are announced first, then the other guests come down and select a gift.

If you participate in a giveaway and receive a gift, be sure to thank all the members of the sponsoring family. This is usually done with a hand-shake before returning to your seat. Gifts at a giveaway range from horses, which are uncommon, to blankets, clothing, food, and other household goods that are more common.

Meals at Shoshoni public gatherings are known as feasts. It is normal for the sponsors to give any leftover food to guests as they leave. It is not considered rude to take the leftovers home if you are a guest.

Prestige and status in a Shoshoni community can be enhanced by open generosity. A person can show his or her generosity by giving away material goods and wealth at a public gathering, such as the giveaway. Indian people in general share more readily than non-Indian people. There is the expectation of reciprocity involved in sharing among Indians, especially with relatives.

Grammar

gande AND ba'i

There are two words in Shoshoni for the verb "to have": **gande** and **ba'i**. Neither word is used like the verb "to have" in English.

The possessor comes first (I, my mother), then the possessed object (dog, house), and then either **gande** or **ba'i**. Although there is no difference in their meanings, the form **gande** is more common among Shoshoni speakers in Nevada, while the form **ba'i** is more common among Shoshoni speakers in Idaho and Wyoming.

Ne sadee' gande. I have a dog.
Ne sadee' ba'i. I have a dog.
Ne bia' gahni gande. My mother has a house.
Ne bia' gahní ba'i. My mother has a house.

To negate these examples simply place the word **gai** ("not") in front of the possessed object (dog, house).

Ne gai sadee' gande. I don't have a dog.
Ne gai sadee' ba'i. I don't have a dog.
Ne bia' gai gahni gande. My mother doesn't have a house.
Ne bia' gai gahní ba'i. My mother doesn't have a house.

Questions are constructed with **gande** and **ba'i** by placing the question particle **ha** after the possessor (you, your mother).

Enne ha sadee' gande? Do you have a dog?
Enne ha sadee' ba'i? Do you have a dog?
Enne ha gai sadee' gande? Don't you have a dog?
Enne ha gai sadee' ba'i? Don't you have a dog?
Em bia' ha gahni gande? Does your mother have a house?
Em bia' ha gahní ba'i? Does your mother have a house?
Em bia' ha gai gahni gande? Doesn't your mother have a house?
Em bia' ha gai gahní ba'i? Doesn't your mother have a house?

Notice that some words change their accent when used before **ba'i** but not before **gande**. For example, **gahní ba'i** versus **gahni gande**

TRANSITIVE AND INTRANSITIVE VERBS

It is important when learning another language to know which verbs can take objects and which cannot. The action of transitive verbs involves some kind of object. Examples of transitive verbs and their objects are to eat dinner, to play the flute, and to throw a ball. Intransitive verbs do not involve any actions with an object. Two intransitive verbs are to sleep, because one does not sleep anything, and to go, because one does not go anything. In the Vocabularies, transitive verbs will be marked [tr] and intransitive verbs will be marked [intr].

THE VERB "TO BE"

In Shoshoni the verb "to be" is a special case, different from all other verbs. It is absent in Shoshoni sentences when it expresses the present tense (I am, you are, etc.).

Ne sosoni'. I'm Shoshoni.
Ne bia' baki'ehe'. My mother is Blackfoot.

Notice that there is a pause between **bia'** and **baki'ehe'** in the second sentence above.

OBJECT CASE OF NOUNS

There are two types of objects: direct objects and indirect objects. Direct objects are the objects upon which the action of the verb is directed. Indirect objects are objects, such as persons or things, that benefit from the action of the verb. The verb does not necessarily act directly upon the indirect object. For example, in the sentence "Mary is baking a cake for Bob," the cake is the direct object because it is the object receiving the action of Mary's baking. "Bob" is the indirect object because Bob is the one who benefits from Mary baking the cake.

All nouns in Shoshoni have a special form that shows that it is the direct object of a verb. Known as the "object case" of nouns, there are seven different ways of forming it in Shoshoni.

1) Some nouns do not change at all for the object case. One example of such a word is **gahni** ("house"). Most of the nouns that do not change already end in "**i**."

2) Otherwise, there are five different suffixes that can be added to form the object case of nouns:

-**a** as in **bia'a** mother
-**ha** as in **dezo'woiha** hat
-**na** as in **guchuna** cow
-**i** as in **bai'** water (from **baa'**)
-**ta** as in **waapita** (Utah) juniper tree, "cedar" tree

Note that the suffix -**i,** too, is sometimes added to the subject case form, as in **bungui** (from **bungu**) "horse," and sometimes the final vowel of the subject case form of the noun is deleted first before the -**i** suffix is added, as in **bungi** (from **bungu**) "horse," or **newi** (from **newe**) "person," "Indian," "Shoshoni Indian."

Note, also, that the suffix -**ai** is also added after deleting the final vowel of the subject case form of the noun, as in **nanihai** (from **naniha**) "name" or **yambai** (from **yamba**) "wild carrots." The following is a list of all of the possible suffix forms that the object case of nouns can take in Shoshoni:

-ø (no suffix)
-**ta**
-**a**
-**i**
-**ha**
-**ai**
-**na**

The object case ending of nouns will be indicated in the Vocabularies. The following is a list of all the nouns used so far with their object case forms:

ape′ ape′a father
ada′ ada′a uncle (maternal)
babi′ babi′a elder brother
baha′ baha′a aunt (paternal)
baide′ baide′a daughter
baki′ehe′ baki′ehe′a Blackfoot Indian
banabui′ banabui′a window
bannaite′ bannaite′a Bannock Indian
bazi′ bazi′a older sister
bia′ bia′a mother
daga′ daga′a friend (male)
daiboo′ daiboo′a Euro-American
daigwape daigwapeha language
dai′zhi dai′zhi brother-in-law (man's)
dawi′ dawi′a younger brother
deigu′ deigu′a a little bit
degupita′ degupita′a light (electric)
dogo′ dogo′a grandfather (maternal)
doyadaiboo′ doyadaiboo′a Mexican
dua′ dua′a son
duu-daiboo′ duu-daiboo′a African-American
gadenoo′ gadenoo′a chair
gahni gahni house
gagu′ gagu′a grandmother (maternal)
genu′ genu′a grandfather (paternal)
hainji hainjiha friend (male)
hutsi′ hutsi′a grandmother (paternal)
nadainape′ nadainape′a husband
nammi′ nammi′a younger sister
naniha nanihai name
nawa′aipe′ nawa′aipe′a wife
nazatewa′ nazatewa′a door
newe newi person
newezoiga′i newezoiga′iha Nez Perce Indian
sii-bungudaiboo′ sii-bungudaiboo′a Basque
sosoni′ sosoni′a Shoshoni Indian
tsadamani tsadamaniha Chinese
yamba′i yamba′iha Kiowa Indian
yuuta′ yuuta′a Ute Indian

POSSESSIVE CASE OF NOUNS

The formation of the possessive case of a noun is simple: it involves the addition of a silent "**n**" (**-N**) onto the regular object case suffix. The only exception is the suffix **-ta**, which can optionally be deleted before the addition of the silent "**n**," resulting in two forms: **-taN** and **-N**.

The following lists all of the object case endings and the corresponding possessive case endings:

Object Case Ending	Possessive Case Ending
-ø	**-N**
-a	**-aN**
-ha	**-haN**
-na	**-naN**
-ta	**-N/-taN**
-i	**-iN**
-ai	**-aiN**

Because the possessive case suffixes are completely predictable, the possessive case suffixes are not indicated in the Vocabularies. Here are more examples of possessive case formations:

ne ape'am mu'bii my father's car
Dzoon-han gahni John's house
 wa'aipe'an gwasu'u a woman's dress
ne nadainape'an dezo'woi my husband's hat
guchunan duku beef (literally, cow's flesh)

Notice that the form **bunguN** is irregular because the possessive case suffix **-N** is formed from the subject case rather than the object case form.

WHAT? **HINNI** AND **HINNA**

In Chapter 2 you were introduced to the word **hagai'**, meaning both "what? and "how?" For example: **Enne hagai' nanihade?** "What is your name?" (literally, How are you called?)

The word **hinni** is another way to say "what?" in Shoshoni and is used when asking about an object or abstract thought. **Hinni** is the subject case form and **hinna** is the object case form. The object case form is used to ask questions about the objects of verbs. Here are two examples:

Ishe hinni? What is this?
Hinna enne hanni'yu? What are you doing?

Vocabulary for Drills

baa' (bai') water

bungu (bungui/bungi) horse

deka- to eat

    deká'yu am/are/is eating (PROGRESSIVE ASPECT) (something that takes time to complete, such as a full meal)

    dekáa'yu (PAUSAL FORM)

    dekáfe'nni am/are/is eating (CONTINUATIVE ASPECT) (something that does not take very long, such as eating a snack)

aapo' (-a) apple

degumahannipe (-ha) bread (oven-baked)

saape (-ha) stew

pizza (-ha) pizza

deheya'an duku (duki) deer meat, venison

    deheya' (-a) deer

    duku (duki) meat, flesh; mountain sheep

guyungwi'yaa'an duku (duki) turkey (meat)

    guyungwi'yaa' (-a) turkey (bird)

ha'nnibe (-ha) corn (Indian corn), maize

    ha'nniibe (PAUSAL FORM)

yamba (yamb<u>ai</u>) wild carrots (yampa root)

basigoo' (-a) Indian potatoes (camas root)

agai' (agai') salmon

sadee' (-a) dog

sii-bungu (sii-bungi) sheep

sohobi (-ta) tree

    sohoo'bi (PAUSAL FORM)

waapi (-ta) (Utah) juniper tree, "cedar" tree

wongobi (-ta) pine tree

    wongoo'bi (PAUSAL FORM)

gwasu'uN (-na) dress, skirt, shirt, blouse (both men's and women's clothing) [N class]

dezo'woi (-ha) hat

nambe (-ha) shoe(s) (Eastern Shoshoni: **nampeha**)

guchuN (-na) cow [N class]

tsaa-b<u>ai</u>ngwi (tsaa-b<u>ai</u>ngwi) trout

gedii' (-a) cat

da'ga only, just, but (ADV)

Drill 1

Answer the following question:

    Q: **Hinna ennen deká'yu?**

      A1: **Ne tsiina'a deká'yu.**

      A2: **Ne aapo'a deká'yu.**

      A3: **Ne yuhudegumahannipeha deká'yu.**

      A4: **Ne degumahannipeha deká'yu.**

      A5: **Ne saapeha deká'yu.**

      A6: **Ne pizza-ha deká'yu.**

      A7: **Ne deheya'an duki deká'yu.**

      A8: **Ne guyungwi'yaa'an duki deká'yu.**

      A9: **Ne ha'nnibeha deká'yu.**

      A10: **Ne yamb<u>ai</u> deká'yu.**

      A11: **Ne basigoo'a deká'yu.**

      A12: **Ne agai' deká'yu.**

DRILL 1, ENGLISH TRANSLATION:

    Q: What are you eating?

      A1: I'm eating potatoes.

      A2: I'm eating an apple.

      A3: I'm eating fry bread.

      A4: I'm eating (oven-baked) bread.

      A5: I'm eating stew.

      A6: I'm eating pizza.

      A7: I'm eating venison.

      A8: I'm eating turkey.

      A9: I'm eating corn.

      A10: I'm eating wild carrots.

      A11: I'm eating Indian potatoes.

      A12: I'm eating salmon.

Drill 2

Answer the following question:

    Q: **Hinna enne buika?**

      A1: **Gahni ne buika.**

      A2: **Sadee'a ne buika.**

      A3: **Sii-bungi ne buika.**

      A4: **Sohobita ne buika.**

      A5: **Mu'biiha ne buika.**

A6: **Genu'an gahni ne buika.**

A7: **Waapita ne buika.**

A8: **Wongobita ne buika.**

A9: **Gagu'an gwasu'una ne buika.**

A10: **Ada'an dezo'woiha ne buika.**

A11: **Ne ape'an nambeha ne buika.**

A12: **Guchuna ne buika.**

DRILL 2, ENGLISH TRANSLATION:

Q: What do you see?

A1: I see a house.

A2: I see a dog.

A3: I see a sheep.

A4: I see a tree.

A5: I see a car.

A6: I see grandpa's house.

A7: I see a juniper tree.

A8: I see a pine tree.

A9: I see grandma's dress.

A10: I see uncle's hat.

A11: I see my father's shoes.

A12: I see a cow.

Drill 3

Answer the following question:

Q: **Enne hinnim ba'i?**

(NOTE: **hinni** is pronounced **hinnim** before **ba'i**.)

A1: **Ne tsiina' ba'i.**

A2: **Ne aapo' ba'i.**

A3: **Ne gahni' ba'i.**

A4: **Ne sadee' ba'i.**

A5: **Ne mu'bii ba'i.**

A6: **Ne gwasu'um ba'i.**

A7: **Ne dezo'woi ba'i.**

A8: **Ne nambe ba'i.**

A9: **Ne pizza ba'i.**

A10: **Ne guyungwi'yaa' ba'i.**

A11: **Ne degumahannipe ba'i.**

A12: **Ne saape ba'i.**

end of
Tape 2-a

DRILL 3, ENGLISH TRANSLATION:
    Q: What do you have?
        A1: I have potatoes.
        A2: I have an apple.
        A3: I have a house.
        A4: I have a dog.
        A5: I have a car.
        A6: I have a dress.
        A7: I have a hat.
        A8: I have shoes.
        A9: I have a pizza.
        A10: I have a turkey.
        A11: I have bread.
        A12: I have some stew.

Drill 4

start of Tape 2-b Answer the following questions with both **haa'** ("yes") and **g<u>a</u>i'** ("no"). Answer with complete sentences.

    Q1: **Enne ha aapo' ba'i?**
        1b: **Haa', ne aapo' ba'i.**
        1b: **G<u>a</u>i ne aapo' ba'i, ne tsiina' ba'i da'ga.**
    Q2: **Enne ha tsiina' ba'i?**
        2a: **Haa', ne tsiina' ba'i.**
        2b: **G<u>a</u>i ne tsiina' ba'i, ne yamba ba'i da'ga.**
    Q3: **Enne ha yamba ba'i?**
        3a: **Haa', ne yamba ba'i.**
        3b: **G<u>a</u>i ne yamba ba'i, ne basigoo' ba'i da'ga.**
    Q4: **Enne ha agai' ba'i?**
        4a: **Haa', ne agai' ba'i.**
        4b: **G<u>a</u>i ne agai' ba'i, ne tsaa-b<u>a</u>ingwi ba'i da'ga.**
    Q5: **Enne ha sadee' ba'i?**
        5a: **Haa', ne sadee' ba'i.**
        5b: **G<u>a</u>i ne sadee' ba'i, ne gedii' ba'i da'ga.**
    Q6: **Enne ha guchúm ba'i?**
        6a: **Haa', ne guchúm ba'i.**
        6b: **G<u>a</u>i ne guchúm ba'i, ne guyungwi'yaa' ba'i da'ga.**

DRILL 4, ENGLISH TRANSLATION:

　　Q1: Do you have an apple?

　　　　1a: Yes, I have an apple.

　　　　1b: I don't have an apple, but I have potatoes.

　　Q2: Do you have any potatoes?

　　　　2a: Yes, I have some potatoes.

　　　　2b: I don't have any potatoes, but I have some wild carrots.

　　Q3: Do you have any wild carrots?

　　　　3a: Yes, I have some wild carrots.

　　　　3b: I don't have any wild carrots, but I have some Indian potatoes.

　　Q4: Do you have any salmon?

　　　　4a: Yes, I have some salmon.

　　　　4b: I don't have any salmon, but I have some trout.

　　Q5: Do you have a dog?

　　　　5a: Yes, I have a dog.

　　　　5b: I don't have a dog, but I have a cat.

　　Q6: Do you have a cow?

　　　　6a: Yes, I have a cow.

　　　　6b: I don't have a cow, but I have a turkey.

Drill 5

Answer the following question with the various persons provided:

　　Q: **Enne ha mu'bii ba'i?**

　　　　A1: **Gai', ne ape' da'ga.**

　　　　A2: **Gai', ne bia' da'ga.**

　　　　A3: **Gai', ne genu' da'ga.**

　　　　A4: **Gai', ne hutsi' da'ga.**

　　　　A5: **Gai', ne dua' da'ga.**

　　　　A6: **Gai', ne baide' da'ga.**

　　　　A7: **Gai', ne hainji da'ga.**

　　　　A8: **Gai', ne dei' da'ga.**

　　　　A9: **Gai', ne babi' da'ga.**

　　　　A10: **Gai', ne bazi' da'ga.**

　　　　A11: **Gai', ne dawi' da'ga.**

　　　　A12: **Gai', ne nammi' da'ga.**

DRILL 5, ENGLISH TRANSLATION:

> Q: Do you have a car?
>> A1: No, but my father does.
>> A2: No, but my mother does.
>> A3: No, but my (paternal) grandpa does.
>> A4: No, but my (paternal) grandma does.
>> A5: No, but my son does.
>> A6: No, but my daughter does.
>> A7: No, but my (male) friend does.
>> A8: No, but my (female) friend does.
>> A9: No, but my older brother does.
>> A10: No, but my older sister does.
>> A11: No, but my younger brother does.
>> A12: No, but my younger sister does

5

Haga' ne nambe?
("Where's my shoe?")

- "Where is . . . ?"
- Postpositions
- Adjectives
- Colors
- Verb endings

Vocabulary for Dialog 1

Tape 2-b (cont.)

haga' where?

gapai (gapai) bed

duka under [postpos]

aingabite (aingabiti) red [adj]

da'oda- to find
   da'ota find/finds (DURATIVE ASPECT)

binnangwa behind [postpos] (object is behind something facing the speaker)

nazawaiyiH- to hang [intr] [H class]
   nazawaiyihka am/is/are hanging (RESULTATIVE)

hagadeN [+ noun] which . . . ? [N class]

nado'aigahni (nado'aigahni) bathroom, restroom, toilet (more common among women)

gaH in, at [postpos] [H class]

dapaihyaa' (-a) sock(s)

ba'aN on top of [postpos] [N class]

dapaihyaaH- to put on (one's) socks [H class]
   dapaihyaa' put on your socks! (IMPERATIVE)
   dapáihyahwa put (PAST TENSE) on (one's) socks (MOMENTANEOUS ASPECT)
   -kwa/-hwa (MOMENTANEOUS ASPECT)

73

-kua' go and do something [auxiliary verb]
    dap<u>ái</u>hyaakua' go and put your socks on
dosabite (dosabiti) white [adj]
biagwasu'u (-na) coat
hagannihatu enne nahá'yu? what are you doing?
haganni how? in what way? what? (nonmaterial)
    hagannihatu (ALTERNATE FORM) = **haganni**
naha- to do, to make, to happen [intr]
    nahá'yu am/is/are doing/making (PROGRESSIVE)
    naháa'yu (PAUSAL FORM)
ma it, that, this [object case]
-nei' left to do something and came back [auxiliary verb]
dukai (ALTERNATE FORM) = **duka**
m<u>ai</u> I said, people say, they say (QUOTATIVE PARTICLE)
niikwi- to tell, to say
    niikwi said, told (MOMENTANEOUS ASPECT)
b<u>ai</u>sheN already [N class]
g<u>ai</u>yu'uN late [N class]
nukíndema just go then! (EXPRESSION)
    nuki- to run [intr]
    demma/demmase then$TOP

Dialog 1

Dennis and his older sister, Mary, are at home getting ready for school. Their mother is sitting in the living room watching TV.
    Dennis (holding one shoe): **Mom, haga' ne nambe?**
    Mom: **En gap<u>ai</u> duka.**

Dennis leaves and Mary enters the room.
    Mary: **Mom, haga'a'nna ude <u>ai</u>ngabite ne gwasu'u? Ne g<u>ai</u> u da'ota.**
    Mom: **Nazatewa' binnangwa, nazaw<u>ai</u>yihka.**
    Mary: **Hagaden nazatewa' binnangwa?**
    Mom: **Nado'<u>ai</u>gahni ga.**

Mary leaves. Dennis enters the room wearing his shoes without any socks.
    Mom: **Dennis, haga' en dap<u>ai</u>hyaa'?**
    Dennis: **Ne gap<u>ai</u> ba'a.**
    Mom: **U dap<u>ái</u>hyaakua'.**

Dennis leaves and Mary enters the room.

Mary: **Mom, haga' uden dosabiten ne biagwasu'u?**

Mom: **Mu'bii gupa.**

Mary goes to get her coat. Dennis enters the room with his socks over his shoes.

Mom (with an angry voice): **Hagannihatu ennen nahá'yu?**

Dennis: **Ne ma dapáihyaanei'.**

Mom: **En nambe dukai ma dapáihyaakua' mai ne en niikwi.**

Dennis: **Ne baishen gaiyu'un nahá'yu.**

Mom: **Nukíndemma!**

ENGLISH TRANSLATION:

Dennis (holding one shoe): Mom, where's my shoe?

Mom: It's under your bed.

Dennis leaves and Mary enters the room.

Mary: Mom, where's my red dress? I can't find it.

Mom: It's hanging up behind the door.

Mary: Behind which door?

Mom: In the bathroom.

Mary leaves. Dennis enters the room wearing his shoes without any socks.

Mom: Dennis, where are your socks?

Dennis: On top of my bed.

Mom: Go and put them on your feet.

Dennis leaves and Mary enters the room.

Mary: Mom, where's my white coat?

Mom: It's inside the car.

Mary goes to get her coat. Dennis enters the room with his socks over his shoes.

Mom (with an angry voice): What are you doing?

Dennis: I went and put them on.

Mom: I meant on your feet under your shoes and not over your shoes.

Dennis: But I'm already late.

Mom: Just go then!

LITERAL TRANSLATION:

D: Mom, where my shoe?

Mo: Your bed under.

Dennis leaves and Mary enters the room.

 Ma: Mom, where that red my dress? I not it find(durative).

 Mo: Door behind hanging-(resultative).

 Ma: Which door behind?

 Mo: Bathroom in.

Mary leaves. Dennis enters the room wearing his shoes without any socks.

 Mo: Dennis, where your sock?

 D: My bed on=top.

 Mo: It put=on=socks-go=and=do.

 Ma: Mom, where that white my coat?

 Mo: Car inside.

Mary goes to get her coat. Dennis enters the room with his socks over his shoes.

 Mo (with an angry voice): What you doing-(progressive)?

 D: I that put=on=socks-did=and=came.

 Mo: Your shoe under-(object case) that put=on=socks-go=and=do
  quotative-particle I you told-(momentaneous).

 D: I already late doing-(progressive).

 Mo: Run-then!

Vocabulary for Dialog 2

 uka [object case] of **udeN**

 duhubiti [object case] of **duhubite**

 gusai [object case] of **gusa**

 haga'ahku (alternative form) of **haga'a'nna**

 bunni- to happen to see (tr), to see by chance

  bu'nni happened to see, saw by chance(DURATIVE)

 beaichehkuseN in the morning, early [adv] [N class]

 ba'angu (alternative form) of **ba'aN**

 gaiháiwa'i it's not there (expression), there's nothing there

 ba'ande (alternative form) of **ba'aN**

 gahti (alternative form) of **gaH**

 sabai in there

  saa'bai (PAUSAL FORM)

 tsategi- to put (something) by hand [tr]

  u tsatéginei' went and put it (and has/have returned; pronounced [**uzatégiyei'**])

 tso'ape (-ha) ghost

gia' maybe, perhaps

seba maybe, perhaps

   see'ba (PAUSAL FORM)

sebagia' maybe, perhaps

giaséba maybe, perhaps

   giasée'ba (PAUSAL FORM)

bituseN back [adv] (as in "to give back") [N class]

tsa'uhtu"- to give (something) by hand [G class] [tr]

   tsa- by hand/with the hands [instrumental pref]

   utu"- to give [G class]

bituseN . . . tsa'uhtukwa gave back, returned (something) (MOMEN-
TANEOUS ASPECT) [N class]

ma̱iku okay, alright

ege- new (prefixed to noun)

gwasu'uN (-na) blouse; shirt (men's or women's); dress, skirt [N
class]

a̱ishimbite (a̱ishimbiti) grey

niigwi'nna telling, saying (to) (ITERATIVE ASPECT)(from **niikwi-**)

mi'awa'iH- to go out (from **mi'a-**) [H class]

   mi'awa'ihyu going out (PROGRESSIVE)

ga̱i demase hagapundu mi'ade Stay home then! [polite negative
imperative] (literally, don't go anywhere then)

Dialog 2

Mary is at home getting ready to go out to a movie with her friends. Her
mom is in the living room watching TV.

   Mary (enters the living-room): **Mom, enne ha uka duhubiti nean
gusa̱i ga̱i haga'aku bu'nni?**

   Mom: **Ne bea̱ichehkuse, emmen gapa̱i ba'angu u buikwa.**

   Mary: **Ga̱iháiwa'i, u ba'ande.**

   Mom: **Enne ha nado'a̱igahni gahti buinei'?**

   Mary: **Hagade saba̱i u tsatéginei'?**

   Mom: **Tso'ape gia' se'ba.**

Mary leaves the room and returns wearing her black pants.

   Mom: **Haga'ahku enne ma da'odanei'?**

   Mary: **Uden tso'ape bitusen ne gusa̱i ne tsa'utukwa. Ma̱iku, enne
ha ne ege-gwasu'una ga̱i haga'aku bu'nni?**

   Mom: **Ege-gwasu'u?**

   Mary: **Ude a̱ishimbite.**

   Mom: **Ne ga̱i en niigwi'nna sumbana'i'nna, ne ga̱i u buide.**

Mary: **Ne g̲ai hagapundu mi'awa'ihyu ne ege-gwasu'una g̲ai da'o-dade.**

Mom: **M̲aiku, g̲ai demase hagapundu mi'ade.**

ENGLISH TRANSLATION:

Mary (enters the living room): Mom, have you seen my black pants?

Mom: I saw them on your bed this morning.

Mary: But they're not there now.

Mom: Did you look in the bathroom?

Mary: Well, who put them in there?

Mom: Maybe it was a ghost.

Mary leaves the room and returns wearing her black pants.

Mom: Where did you find them?

Mary: The ghost gave them back to me. But have you seen my new blouse?

Mom: Which new blouse?

Mary: The grey one.

Mom: I don't know. I haven't seen it lately.

Mary: I can't go out without my new blouse.

Mom: Alright, stay home then.

LITERAL TRANSLATION:

Ma: Mom, you question-particle that-(object case) black-(object case) my pants-(object case) not somewhere saw(durative).

Mo: I early, your bed on=top saw-(momentaneous).

Ma: Absent, it on=top.

Mo: You question-particle bathroom to see-did=and=came

Ma: Who there it put-did=and=came?

Mo: Ghost maybe perhaps.

Mo: Where-(object case) you that find-did=and=came.

Mary leaves the room and returns wearing her black pants.

Ma: That ghost back my pants-(object case) me put-(momentaneous). Okay, you question-particle my new-dress-(object case) not somewhere saw (durative)?

Mo: New-dress?

Ma: That grey.

Mo: I not you telling-(iterative) not=know, I not it see-(habitual).

Ma: I not where going=out-(progressive) I new-dress-(object case) not find-(habitual).

Mo: Okay, not then where go-(habitual).

Language and Culture

CODE-SWITCHING

"Code-switching" involves bilingual people mixing languages to some degree. Do not be surprised if English words and phrases are mixed in Shoshoni conversation, especially when talking to people who understand both languages. Since most Shoshoni speakers are bilingual in English, one can code-switch into English when one can't remember the Shoshoni word.

Code-switching can occur in any of the following three ways:

1) speakers can switch languages between sentences,
2) speakers can switch languages in the middle of a sentence, and
3) speakers can intersperse one language with words from the other.

Code-switching is triggered within a conversation by any of three factors:

1) the place where the conversation takes place—some localities require the use of a particular language,

2) the topic under discussion—some topics require the use of a particular language, and

3) the audience—we tend to use a particular language with certain people.

Some people are "language purists" who believe that code-switching is bad. They claim that it weakens a language or that people are beginning to lose their language. Code-switching more often than not indicates that, even though speakers are bilingual, they tend to speak on some topics more easily in one language than in the other.

Grammar

MORE ON POSTPOSITIONS

Postpositions already introduced are (from Chapter 2): **gahtu, nai', naite, ma'ai**; (from Chapter 3): **duN, ba'ande**; (from Chapter 4): **gupaN, dukaN, ma'i**; (from Dialog 1 in this chapter): **binnangwa, gaH, ba'aN, dukai**; (from Dialog 2 in this chapter): **ba'angu and gahti**; (from the Drills in this chapter): **maa'nangwa, gewaga, wenanga, baihyugi**, and **gupángu**.

There are six basic postpositions that express location in Shoshoni:

ba'aN on top of
dukaN under
gaH in; at; on
gabaN among, between; through
gupaN in, inside; within
maN on; with (instrument)

Notice that the final feature in **gaH** is the aspirating final feature (**-H**), and that **gaH** is listed in the glossaries with its final feature attached although it is never pronounced when by itself. All words that end in the aspirating final feature will be indicated with (**-H**).

Locative postpositions show location and can themselves take a suffix known as a "postpositional adjunct," which adds a further nuance to the basic meaning of the postposition.

There are five postpositional adjuncts: **-i, -ku, -tuN, -teN,** and **-ti.** Notice that when **-ku, -tuN, -teN,** and **-ti** are added to postpositions that end in a silent "**n**" (the final feature **-N**), these adjuncts will become **-gu, -duN, -deN,** and **-di.**

THE POSTPOSITIONAL ADJUNCT **-i**

The postpositional adjunct **-i** is added to a locative postposition when it describes something that is the grammatical object of the main verb of the sentence. For example, in Dialog 1, Dennis's mom says to him, **en nambe dukai ma dapáihyaakua'**, meaning that she meant for him to put his socks on his feet under his shoes. The postposition takes the adjunct **-i** because **en nambe duka** ("under your shoes") is used to describe what is also the object of the verb (**ma,** "it" or "that"; that is, the socks). Words or phrases that describe the object of the verb in Shoshoni usually end with some form of the object case ending.

A second usage of the postpositional adjunct **-i** (not illustrated in this chapter) is with an intransitive verb of motion (a verb that describes some kind of movement and does not take an object). The implicative or implied nuance of meaning is that the movement occurs only within a specified area.

THE POSTPOSITIONAL ADJUNCT **-ku**

The postpositional adjunct **-ku** is added to the locative postposition of any locative postpositional phrase stating where someone or something is that is the object of the verb "to see." For example, in Dialog 2, Mary's mom says to her, **ne be<u>ai</u>chehkuse, emmen gap<u>ai</u> ba'angu u buikwa** ("I saw it [her black pants] on your bed this morning"). The postposition **ba'aN** ("on top of") takes the adjunct **-ku** to show that it describes **u** ("it"), the object of the verb **buikwa** ("saw").

Another usage of the postpositional adjunct **-ku** is with a transitive verb showing movement (a verb that takes an object and indicates motion). The implied nuance of meaning is that the movement is toward a specified area.

THE POSTPOSITIONAL ADJUNCT -teN

The postpositional adjunct **-teN** is added to a locative postposition when the locative phrase that the postposition is a part of describes an object that is at rest and not the object of a verb of motion. In the following examples the locative phrase **ba'ande** ("on top of") describes an object at rest that is not the direct object of a verb: (1) using the postposition **ba'aN**, Duffy, in Chapter 3, Dialog 2, asked her grandmother, <u>ai</u>de **wihyu daha-ba'ande?** ("What about that above the two of us?"), to refer to the ceiling light above both of them; (2) in Dialog 2 of this chapter, Mary's response to her mother after hearing her mother say that the last place she saw Mary's black pants was on top of her bed is **gaih<u>á</u>iwa'i, u ba'ande** ("there's nothing there, on top of it [the bed]").

Another example of this adjunct is the word **naite** ("from" [a specific, named location]), which should be considered an idiosyncratic usage of this adjunct at this point.

THE POSTPOSITIONAL ADJUNCT -tuN

The postpositional adjunct **-tuN** is added to locative postpositions that are used with intransitive verbs indicating movement, that is, verbs that describe motion and do not take an object. The implied nuance of meaning is that of movement to, into, or through a specified area. For example, with the postposition **gaH**, in Chapter 2, Dialog 1, when Sue is asked where she is going, she responds, **gahni gahtu** ("to home"). Notice that the postposition **gaH** means "in," "at," or "on," but when the adjunct **-tu** is added to it, it takes on the meaning of "to," "into," or "through."

THE POSTPOSITIONAL ADJUNCT **-ti**

The postpositional adjunct **-ti** is added to locative postpositions that occur in locative phrases describing an object that is the object of a transitive verb and is also moving. For example, in Dialog 2 of this chapter, Mary's mom asks her, **enne ha nado'<u>ai</u>gahni gahti buinei'?** ("did you go and look [for the black pants] in the bathroom?"). Notice that in this instance **gahti** can be translated as "into . . . " and "out of . . . " and is used because the verb **bui-** ("to see") involves movement when used with the verbal auxiliary **-nei'** ("to go and [do something]").

ADJECTIVES

Adjectives are used to describe nouns and pronouns, such as the car is "green," they are "tall," and it is "intergalactic." There are three fundamentally different types or classes of adjectives in Shoshoni.

One type of adjective is only used prefixed to the noun it describes. Prefixed adjectives describe an attribute of the noun, and are attached directly to the noun, as in **ege-gwasu'u** ("new blouse"). Notice that (1) prefixed adjectives have to be prefixed to a noun and cannot be used predicatively (that is, following the verb of a sentence) to describe a noun (such as "that man is bad" or "the house is small") and (2) prefixed adjectives do not change in case or number.

There are two classes of freestanding adjectives in Shoshoni. The first class is known as "true adjectives." True adjectives end in one of seven adjectival endings or suffixes. One adjectival suffix already introduced is **-teN**. True adjectives change the suffix ending to **-ti** in the object case, that is, when the adjective is describing a noun which is the object of the verb in that sentence. For example:

> **Sadee' duhubite.** The dog is black.
> **Sadee'a duhubiti ne buika.** I see a black dog.

In the second sentence the adjective **duhubiti** ends in the object case ending **-ti** since it describes the dog, which itself is the object of the speaker's observance and therefore also in the object case (**sadee'a**). Notice also that it doesn't matter whether the adjective comes before or after the noun when used predicatively.

The second class of adjectives is known as "nominal adjectives." Nominal adjectives are nouns that are used like adjectives to describe other nouns. English uses such nouns as "vacation house" where the noun "vacation" is used to describe the type of house. When a nominal adjective is used to describe a noun that is in the object case, it will take the usual object case endings appropriate to nouns. Nominal adjectives are all those adjectives that do not end in **-te** or **-ti**.

For example, the word for the color "pink" is **ainga'aibi**. This adjective is the only color term that is not a true adjective and takes the object case ending **-ta** (**ainga'aibita**).

COLORS

All the colors, except for "pink," are true adjectives in Shoshoni and end in the adjectival suffix: **-bite** (**-biti** [object case]). The word for "pink" is the only exception because it is a noun and takes the object case suffix **-ta** (**ainga'aibita**). The Shoshoni colors correspond closely to their English equivalents. The primary color terms are:

> **duhubite** black
> **dosabite** white
> **aishimbite** grey
> **ondembite** brown
> **aikwehibite** purple
> **aibehibite** blue
> **buhibite** green
> **ohapite** yellow
> **aingabite** red
> **ainga'aibi'** pink

THE FUTURE TENSE IN ENGLISH AND SHOSHONI

Shoshoni verb endings are not as concerned with "when" an event occurred, as they are in English, but more with "how" an event occurred. There are two verbal suffixes in Shoshoni that correspond to the English future tense: **-du'i** (FUTURE TENSE) and **-nuhi** (EXPECTIVE TENSE). The main difference between the two is that the expectative tense is less certain the action of the verb will occur than it is in the future tense. If there is any doubt that an action might occur, use the expective tense; otherwise you can use the future tense. For example:

> **Ne binnagwasen dekadu'i.** I am going to eat later.
> **Ne binnagwasen dekanuhi.** I expect to eat later.

THE PAST TENSE IN ENGLISH AND SHOSHONI

In Shoshoni there are three verbal suffixes that correspond to the English past tense: **-nnu** (COMPLETIVE ASPECT), **-ku/-kwa** (MOMENTANEOUS ASPECT), and the auxiliary verbal suffix **-ki**.

First of all, the main difference between the completive aspect (**-nnu**) and the momentaneous aspect (**-ku/-kwa**) is that the completive aspect stresses that the action of the verb is completed, while the momentaneous aspect implies that the action of the verb is completed and took only a very short period of time to occur. For example, for any actions that occurred quickly and then were over, use the momentaneous aspect (**-ku/-kwa**). For actions that occurred over a period of time or have been completed for a while, use the completive aspect (**-nnu**).

Another difference is that the momentaneous aspect involves some kind of movement on the part of either the subject(s) and/or object(s) of the verb; the completive aspect shows a lack of movement on the part of the subject(s) and/or object(s) of the verb. For example, in the first sentence movement is implied (most likely the speaker was moving), while in the second there is no movement:

Ne sohobita buinnu. I saw a tree.
Ne sohobita buikwa. I saw a tree.

The auxiliary verbal suffix **-ki** is added to a verb stem and gives it the meaning of "just arrived and [verb]-ed" or "just [verb]-ed." Two other auxiliary verbal suffixes are **-nei'** and **-kua'**. These two suffixes are discussed below in the section on auxiliary verbs.

THE PRESENT TENSE IN ENGLISH AND SHOSHONI

There are seven verbal suffixes in Shoshoni that correspond to the English present tense: **-'yu** (PROGRESSIVE ASPECT), **-fe'nni/-pe'nni** (CONTINUATIVE ASPECT), **-ka** (RESULTATIVE ASPECT), **-deN** (HABITUAL-CUSTOMARY ASPECT), **-'nna** (ITERATIVE ASPECT), **-ge'nna** (REPETITIVE ASPECT), and finally the (DURATIVE ASPECT) that is signaled by the hardening of an internal consonant in the verb stem (for example, **hapí** from the verb stem **habi-** "to lie").

These seven Shoshoni verbal suffixes correspond to four groups of English present tense forms:

1) The progressive aspect (**-'yu**) and the continuative aspect (**-fe'nni/ -pe'nni**) correspond to the English present progressive ("is/are [verb]-ing"). The main difference is that the progressive aspect is used for ac-

tions that take longer and the continuative aspect is used for actions that are shorter in duration.

2) The resultative aspect (**-ka**) and the customary-habitual aspect (**-deN**) are used to show action that regularly occurs over a long period of time. The difference is that the resultative aspect is used to show that the action of the verb is the result of some prior action. The customary-habitual aspect is used to show that an action is done on a customary or habitual basis over a period of time.

3) The iterative aspect (**-'nna**) and the repetitive aspect (**-ge'nna**) are used to show repeated action. The iterative aspect is used to show repeated action that occurred more quickly, and the repetitive aspect is used to show repeated action that occurred slowly. Also, the iterative aspect can be used to show that the action of the verb is a result of a prior action, similar to the resultitive aspect.

4) The durative aspect shows that the action of the verb lasted for a period of time and stresses the duration of the action. The durative aspect does not involve a suffix. Instead, there is an internal sound change that involves the hardening of a soft consonant between two vowels within the verb stem. For example, **da'ota** ("find/finds") from **da'oda-**, or **gaté** ("sit/sits") from **gade-**. Notice that not all verb stems can take every verbal suffix. It is best to stick to the forms you actually hear. Memorize examples of usage in the form of phrases or dialogs.

IMPERATIVES

The imperative form of a verb is a direct command. The imperative form in Shoshoni is the stem of the verb by itself. For example, in Chapter 4, Dialog 1, Grandma uses a direct imperative when she tells Dennis to bring her the frying pan: **degwasenge'a tsayaahki.** The imperative form is made with the verb stem **tsayaahki-** "to carry (something) down low using both hands." All languages have different levels of politeness. You must be careful when using the direct imperative form of a verb in Shoshoni. Depending on the situation, the imperative form could be interpreted as rude. Avoid using the direct imperative form with people older than yourself and with people who deserve respect because of their status in the community, such as religious and community leaders, teachers, healers, etc. For example, in the dialog, the grandmother uses the imperative form with her grandson because he is younger.

The negative imperative ("don't [verb]") is formed by putting **gai** ("not") in front of the verb and by adding the customary-habitual suffix (**-deN**). For example, in Dialog 2 Mary's mom tells her: **gai demase**

hagapundu mi'ade "don't go out anywhere then!" The negative imperative form can be as impolite as the direct imperative form!

Another way of constructing the imperative form is with the auxiliary verb **-kua'**. (Refer to the next section for more information.)

THE AUXILIARY VERBS **-kua'**, **-nei'**, AND **-ki**

Auxiliary verbs in Shoshoni are suffixes that are added onto a regular verb stem. No other tense/aspect suffixes are added after the auxiliary verbs. Two auxiliary verbs already introduced in this chapter are **-kua'** and **-nei'**. The auxiliary **-ki** is introduced in the Drills section below.

The auxiliary verb **-kua'** is a suffix used with a verb stem meaning "go and do [verb]." For example, in Dialog 1, Dennis's mom tells him to go and put his socks on his feet: **u dapáihyaakua'**. The auxiliary verb **-kua'** can also be used as a command form since it implies that the action of the verb is yet to be completed.

The auxiliary verb **-nei'** implies that the action of the verb stem to which it is attached has already been completed. It specifically means: "left to do [verb], completed [verb], and came back." For example, in Dialog 2, Mary's mom asks her if she looked in the bathroom for her black pants: **enne ha nado'aigahni gahti buinei'?** Mary's mother uses the auxiliary verb **-nei'** to imply that Mary would have to have left the room and gone to the bathroom, and then returned in order to know whether her pants are still there or not. In another example from the same dialog, Mary's mom asks her where she found her pants. Mary's mother again uses the auxiliary verb **-nei'**: **haga'aku enne ma da'odanei'?** In this example, **-nei'** implies that Mary has gone somewhere (since she left the room for a while) and then returned, having found her pants in the meantime.

Notice that when the stem of the verb does not end in a final feature (-ø), the "**n**" in **-nei'** becomes a nasalized "**y**" (that is, air comes out of both your mouth and nose). This change in pronunciation also occurs in the following words: **buinei'** [**buiyei'**], **tsatéginei'** [**tsatégiyei'**], and **da'odanei'** [**da'odayei'**].

The auxiliary verb **-ki** means "just arrived and [verb]-ed" or "just [verb]-ed." In this chapter's Drill section, **-ki** is added to **bui-** ("to see") to mean "saw X and just arrived."

INSTRUMENTAL PREFIXES

In Shoshoni there are a number of prefixes that are added onto the stems of verbs. One group of prefixes, such as the "instrumental prefixes," signals information on how an action was carried out or accomplished. In this lesson you have met the instrumental prefix **tsa"-**, which means "with the hand (using the fingers)". The verb **tegi-** by itself means "to put," but when the instrumental prefix **tsa"-** is added (**tsategi-**), the meaning becomes "to put (something) by hand." Other instrumental prefixes you will meet in this course are: **ba-** "with water" as in **baazagaiH-** "to sprinkle, rain lightly"; **do"-** "with the hand or fist forcefully" as in **domahanni"-** "to knead (dough)"; **ge"-** "with the mouth or by biting" as in **gesunga-** "to taste," "to like (something) by tasting"; **gu"-** "with heat" as in **gutseniH-** "to heat up, get hot"; **ma-** "with the hands" as in **mabizhiaN-** "to fix (something) by hand"; **ni"-** "with the voice" as in **niikwi-** "to say, tell"; **suN-** "with the mind" as in **suwai-** "to want, need"; and **we"-** "with a long instrument" as in **wepagu'i-** "to chop, split (wood, etc.)." As your vocabulary increases, be on the lookout for new words (usually verbs, but sometimes even nouns and adjectives!) that contain these prefixes. This will help you not only in learning to recognize the various parts that Shoshoni words can be broken into but also in discovering the meanings of new words you come across by breaking them down in this way.

Vocabulary for Drills

hagaiti (alternative form) of **hagai'** (refers to a postpositional phrase in the object case)
ohapite (ohapiti) yellow
aibehibite (aibehibiti) blue
buhibite (buhibiti) green
ondembite (ondembiti) brown
ainga'aibi' (ainga'aibita) pink
aikwehibite (aikwehibiti) purple
ainga- red [adj pref]
nabuiN- to be seen, be, look (like) [passive] [N class]
  nabuinde is, looks (like), is seen (CUSTOMARY-HABITUAL ASPECT)
maanangwaH behind [postpos] [H class] (object which is behind something and is also facing away from the speaker)
  maa'nangwaH (PAUSAL FORM)
gewagaH next to, beside [postpos] [H class]
  gewaa'gaH (PAUSAL FORM)
habi- to lie, be (in a supine position)
  hapí am/are/is lying (in a supine position) (DURATIVE ASPECT)
maitengaH outside [adv] [H class]

wenangwaH in front of [postpos] [H class]
ba̲ihyugi next to, beside [postpos]
wene- to stand
   we'nne am/are/is standing (DURATIVE)
gade- to sit
   gaté am/are/is sitting (DURATIVE)
gupángu (alternative form) of **gupa**
ne buiki I saw (something) and have just arrived
   buiki saw (something) and just arrived
   -ki [verb]-ed and just arrived (this suffix indicates the speaker
     has just arrived, and completed the action of the verb
     sometime in the past)
maitengahku (alternative form) of **maitengaH**
maanangwahku (alternative form) of **maanangwaH**
   maa'nangwahku (PAUSAL FORM)
wenangwahku (alternative form) of **wenangwaH**
dukangu (alternative form) of **dukaN**
gewagahku (alternative form) of **gewagaH**

Drill 1

Answer the following question using different colors:
  Q: **Hagaiti ennen gwasú'um ba'i?**
    A1: **Nean gwasu'un duhubite.**
    A2: **Nean gwasu'un dosabite.**
    A3: **Nean gwasu'u a̲ingabite.**
    A4: **Nean gwasu'u a̲ishimbite.**
    A5: **Nean gwasu'u ohapite.**
    A6: **Nean gwasu'u a̲ibehibite.**
    A7: **Nean gwasu'um buhibite.**
    A8: **Nean gwasu'u ondembite.**
    A9: **Nean gwasu'u a̲inga'aibi'.**
    A10: **Nean gwasu'u a̲ikwehibite.**

DRILL 1, ENGLISH TRANSLATION:
  Q: What is the color of your dress/shirt?
    A1: My dress/shirt is black.
    A2: My dress/shirt is white.
    A3: My dress/shirt is red.
    A4: My dress/shirt is grey.
    A5: My dress/shirt is yellow.

A6: My dress/shirt is blue.
A7: My dress/shirt is green.
A8: My dress/shirt is brown.
A9: My dress/shirt is pink.
A10: My dress/shirt is purple.

Drill 2

Answer the following question using different colors:
Q: **Emmem mu'bii hagai' nabuinde?**
A1: **Neam mu'bii duhubite.**
A2: **Neam mu'bii dosabite.**
A3: **Neam mu'bii aingabite.**
A4: **Neam mu'bii aishimbite.**
A5: **Neam mu'bii ohapite.**
A6: **Neam mu'bii aibehibite.**
A7: **Neam mu'bii buhibite.**
A8: **Neam mu'bii ondembite.**
A9: **Neam mu'bii ainga'aibi'.**
A10: **Neam mu'bii aikwehibite.**

DRILL 2, ENGLISH TRANSLATION:
Q: What color is your car?
A1: My car is black.
A2: My car is white.
A3: My car is red.
A4: My car is grey.
A5: My car is yellow.
A6: My car is blue.
A7: My car is green.
A8: My car is brown.
A9: My car is pink.
A10: My car is purple.

Drill 3

Mary describes her different dresses and where they are to her mother.
Ne ainga-gwasu'un, gapai ba'a, or Aingabite ne gwasu'u, gapai' ba'a.
Aibehibite ne gwasu'un, gapai duka.
Buhibite ne gwasu'un, gapaim maa'nangwa.
Ude ne gwasu'u, ainga'aibi', gapain gewaga hapi'.
Aikwehibite ne gwasu'u, gapain gewaga hapi'.

DRILL 3, ENGLISH TRANSLATION:
My red dress is on top of the bed.
My blue dress is under the bed.
My green dress is behind the bed.
My pink dress is next to the bed (lying on the floor).
My purple dress is near the bed (lying on the floor).

Drill 4

Answer the following question.
Q: **Dennis haga'a'nna?**
A1: **Dennis gahni gupa.**
A2: **Dennis maitenga.**
A3: **Dennis gahnim maa'nangwa.**
A4: **Dennis gahni wenangwa.**
A5: **Dennis gahni ba'a.**
A6: **Dennis gahni duka.**
A7: **Dennis gahni b<u>ai</u>hyugi.**
A8: **Dennis gahni b<u>ai</u>hyugi we'nne.**
A9: **Dennis gahni b<u>ai</u>hyugi gaté.**

DRILL 4, ENGLISH TRANSLATION:
Q: Where is Dennis?
A1: Dennis is in the house.
A2: Dennis is outside.
A3: Dennis is behind the house.
A4: Dennis is in front of the house.
A5: Dennis is on top of the house.
A6: Dennis is under the house.
A7: Dennis is next to the house.
A8: Dennis is standing next to the house.
A9: Dennis is sitting next to the house.

Drill 5

Answer the following question:
Q: **Dennis haga'a'nna?**
A1: **Gahni gupangu ne u buiki.**
A2: **Gahni gupangu ne u buikwa.**
A3: **Gahni gupangu ne u buinnu.**
A4: **Gahni gupangu ne u buniku.**

A5: **Ne maitengahku u buiki.**
A6: **Ne maitengahku u buikwa.**
A7: **Ne maitengahku u buinnu.**
A8: **Ne maitengahku u buniku.**
A9: **Gahnim maa'nangwahku ne u buiki.**
A10: **Gahnim maa'nangwahku ne u buikwa.**
A11: **Gahnim maa'nangwahku ne u buinnu.**
A12: **Gahnim maa'nangwahku ne u buniku.**
A13: **Gahni wenangwahku ne u buiki.**
A14: **Gahni wenangwahku ne u buikwa.**
A15: **Gahni wenangwahku ne u buinnu.**
A16: **Gahni wenangwahku ne u buniku.**
A17: **Gahni ba'angu ne u buiki.**
A18: **Gahni ba'angu ne u buikwa.**
A19: **Gahni ba'angu ne u buinnu.**
A20: **Gahni ba'angu ne u buniku.**
A21: **Gahni dukangu ne u buiki.**
A22: **Gahni dukangu ne u buikwa.**
A23: **Gahni dukangu ne u buinnu.**
A24: **Gahni dukangu ne u buniku.**
A25: **Gahnin gewagahku ne u buiki.**
A26: **Gahnin gewagahku ne u buikwa.**
A27: **Gahnin gewagahku ne u buinnu.**
A28: **Gahnin gewagahku ne u buniku.**

end of
Tape 2-b

DRILL 5, ENGLISH TRANSLATION:

Q: Where is Dennis?

A1: I saw him in the house (and I just arrived).
A2: I saw him in the house (and either he or I or both of us were moving).
A3: I saw him in the house (and neither of us were moving).
A4: I happened to see him in the house (I was only glancing and happened to notice him).
A5: I saw him outside (and I just arrived).
A6: I saw him outside (and either he or I or both of us were moving).
A7: I saw him outside (and neither of us were moving).
A8: I happened to see him outside (I was only glancing and happened to notice him).
A9: I saw him behind the house (and I just arrived).

A10: I saw him behind the house (and either he or I or both or us were moving).

A11: I saw him behind the house (and neither of us were moving).

A12: I happened to see him behind the house (I was only glancing and happened to notice him).

A13: I saw him in front of the house (and I just arrived).

A14: I saw him in front of the house (and either he or I or both of us were moving).

A15: I saw him in front of the house (and neither of us were moving).

A16: I happened to see him in front of the house (I was only glancing and happened to notice him).

A17: I saw him on top of the house (and I just arrived).

A18: I saw him on top of the house (and either he or I or both of us were moving).

A19: I saw him on top of the house (and neither of us were moving).

A20: I happened to see him on top of the house (I was only glancing and happened to notice him).

A21: I saw him under the house (and I just arrived).

A22: I saw him under the house (and either he or I or both of us were moving).

A23: I saw him under the house (and neither of us were moving).

A24: I happened to see him under the house (I was only glancing and happened to notice him).

A25: I saw him next to the house (and I just arrived).

A26: I saw him next to the house (and either he or I or both of us were moving).

A27: I saw him next to the house (and neither of us were moving).

A28: I happened to see him next to the house (I was only glancing and happened to notice him)

6

Himb<u>ai</u>'gandei' ennem bungu ba'i?
("How many horses do you have?")

- "How many . . . ?"
- Numbers
- Plural of Nouns, Adjectives, and Verbs

Vocabulary for Dialog 1

start of
Tape 3-a

genú grandfather (paternal) [vocative] (used for calling)
himb<u>ai</u>'gandee' (himb<u>ai</u>'gandei') How many?
    himb<u>ai</u>'gaandee' (PAUSAL FORM)
himb<u>ai</u>'gande How much?
    himb<u>ai</u>'gaande (PAUSAL FORM)
noha used to
manegitee' (manegitei') five (of something) [noun]
egi now
watsewiteese only four
    watsewite (watsewiti) four [numeral]
    -teese only . . . (added to numerals)
biiyaiH- to be left over [H class]
    biiyaihka is/are left over (RESULTATIVE ASPECT)
haganni naakwa? what happened? (pronounced [**haganni yaakwa**])
    naa- to happen; to become; to be; to do (alternate form of **naha-**)
    naakwa happened (MOMENTANEOUS ASPECT)
semme' (-a) one [numeral/noun]
nadewaga- to sell
    nadewagahwa sold (MOMENTANEOUS ASPECT)
himb<u>ai</u>'gandengahtu? for how much (money)?
    himb<u>ai</u>'gaandengahtu (PAUSAL FORM)
    -gahtu for. . . [+ an amount]

wahambiaseemoteN (wahambiaseemoti) two hundred [numeral]

tsugupe' (-a) old man

wahatehwe (wahatehi) two [numeral/noun]

bizhi'-guchuN (-na) milk-cow (specifically female) [N class]

    bizhi' (-a) udder (of cow); breast; milk

noo'yo (noo'yi) testicle

hagai' enne? What do you mean? (literally, what you?)

sudeN that (one) [N class]

gwee' (gwehi) wife

    gwehe (gwehi) [dialect alternative more common in Nevada]

sunni'yunde that's why [conjunction]

oyoseN always [N class]

tsaan deesu'a (it) feels good; (it) has a good outlook

    deesu'a- to feel; to be (in a certain mental state)

    sua- to think

    su'a thinking/think(s) (DURATIVE ASPECT)

Dialog 1

Dennis is visiting his paternal grandparents. He is outside watching his grandfather work.

    Dennis: **Genú? Himbai'gandei' enne bungu ba'i?**

    Genu': **Masen noha manegitee', egi wihyu watsewiteese biiyaihka.**

    Dennis: **Haganni naakwa?**

    Genu': **Semme'a ne nadewagahwa.**

    Dennis: **Himbai'gandengahtu?**

    Genu': **Wahambiaseemotengahtu, ude uka baishen tsugupe'.**

    Dennis: **Enne ha sii-bungu ba'i?**

    Genu': **Gai', wahatehi daga ne bizhi'-guchúm ba'i, semme'a deasen noo'yo gandi.**

    Dennis: **Hagai' enne? Sude ha wahatehi gwee' ba'i?**

    Genu': **Haa', sunni'yunde oyosen tsaan deesu'a.**

ENGLISH TRANSLATION:

    Dennis: Grandpa, how many horses do you have?

    Grandpa: I used to have five, but now I only have four.

    Dennis: What happened?

    Grandpa: I sold one.

    Dennis: For how much?

    Grandpa: For two hundred dollars because it was an old horse.

    Dennis: Do you have any sheep?

Grandpa: No, but I do have two cows and a bull.

Dennis: You mean the bull has two wives?

Grandpa: Yes, that's why he is always happy.

LITERAL TRANSLATION:

D: Grandpa(paternal), how many-(plural/object) you horse have?

G: That used=to=be five-(plural), now then four-only be=left-(resultative)

D: What happened-(momentaneous)?

G: One-(object case) I sold-(momentaneous).

D: How-much-for?

G: Two-big-ten-for, that(invisible) that(invisible/object) already old=man.

D: You question-particle sheep have?

G: No, two-(dual/object) only I milk-cow have one-(object case) also testicle have(object case).

D: How you? That(invisible) question-particle two-(dual/object) wife have?

G: Yes, that's=why always good it=feels(durative)

Vocabulary for Dialog 2

dewee- to buy

    deweedu'i will buy (FUTURE TENSE)

    -du'i (FUTURE TENSE) [verbal suff]

bahaitei' [object case] of **bahaitee'** (three of)

genga (gengai) onion

suwaiH- to want, to need [H class]

    suwaihka want/wants (RESULTATIVE ASPECT), need/needs (RESULTATIVE ASPECT) (implies a large selection of items to choose from)

    suwa'i want/wants (DURATIVE ASPECT), need/needs (DURATIVE ASPECT) (implies only one or two items to choose from)

ukuhti there [adv]

hiwange- to select (from a pile), to pick (things) up (with the hands) [only used with plural objects]

    hiwangekuandu'i will pick (things) up (with the hands)(FUTURE)

o'ohapitee' (o'ohapitei') [pl form] of **ohapite** (yellow)

biaichi' (-a) big [adj]

    bibiaichi' (-a) [pl]

naafaitee' (naafaitei') six of

watsewitee' (watsewitei') four of

tsiambe (-ha) tomato
buhidekape (-ha) (head of) lettuce
tsaandetsi' (-a) nice, little kid (affectionate expression)
duyepe' (-a) boy
sewe (alternative form) of semme' (one)
nadatewaade (nadatewaadi) package, carton
no'yo (no'yi) egg
bizhi'yuhu (bizhi'yuhi) butter
ma'aihku (alternative form) of ma'aiH (with, in addition to)
nade'asengepe (-ha) frozen [adj]; something frozen [noun]
    de'ase- to freeze [tr]

Dialog 2

Dennis is grocery shopping with his paternal grandmother.
    Dennis: **Hutsí? Hinna enne deweedu'i?**
    Hutsi': **Bahaitei', gengai ne suwaihka.**
    Dennis: **Ne ha ukuhti e hiwangekuandu'i?**
    Hutsi': **Bahaitei', o'ohapitei' ne hiwangekua', bibiaichi'a.**
    Dennis: **Hinna enne dease suwaihka?**
    Hutsi': **Ne naafaitei' tsiinna'a, watsewitei' tsiambeha dease**
        semme'a buhidekapeha, suwaihka.

Dennis leaves and then returns with the requested items.
    Dennis: **Hutsí? Iki ma'i.**

He puts the food in her shopping-cart.
    Hutsi': **Ennen tsaandetsi', duyepe'.**
    Dennis: **Hinna dease?**
    Hutsi': **Ne dease sewe nadatewaadi gwi'yaa'an no'yi suwaihka,**
        bizhi'a dease, bizhi'yuhu ma'aihku. Enne wihyu, hinna enne
        suwa'i?
    Dennis: **Pizza-ha nade'asengepeha ne benne suwa'i.**
    Hutsi': **Maiku.**

ENGLISH TRANSLATION:
    Dennis: Grandma, what are going to buy today?
    Grandma: I need three onions.
    Dennis: Can I go get them for you?
    Grandma: Get me three big yellow ones.
    Dennis: What else do you want?
    Grandma: I need six potatoes, four tomatoes, and a head of lettuce.

Dennis leaves and then returns with the requested items.
> Dennis: Here you are, Grandma.

He puts the food in her shopping-cart.
> Grandma: What a nice boy.
> Dennis: What else do you want?
> Grandma: I also need a dozen eggs, milk, and butter. Is there anything you want?
> Dennis: I want frozen pizza.
> Grandma: Okay.

LITERAL TRANSLATION:
> D: Grandma(paternal), what(object) you buy-will?
> G: Three-(pl/object), onion-(object case) I need-(resultative).
> D: I question-particle to-there you pick-(causative)-go-will?
> G: Three-(pl/object), (pl)-yellow-(pl/object) I pick-(causative)-go-and-do, pl)-big-(object case).
> D: What(object) you also need-(resultative)?
> G: I six-(object case) potato-(object case), four-(object case), tomato-(object case), also one-(object case) green-food-(object case), need-(resultative)

Dennis leaves and then returns with the requested items.
> D: Grandma(paternal), here with.

He puts the food in her shopping-cart.
> G: You good-(diminutive), boy.
> D: What also?
> G: I also one box-(object case) chicken-(possessive) egg-(object case) need-(resultative), milk-(object case), also milk-fat with-(object case). You then, what(object) you need-(durative)?
> D: Pizza-(object case) frozen-(object case) I self need-(durative).
> G: Okay.

Grammar

NUMERALS

Numbers in Shoshoni act like nouns. They take case endings, and at times the endings on numbers are similar to dual and plural endings on nouns. The numbers from one to ten are:

semme' (semme'a) one
wahatehwe (wahatehi) two
bah<u>ai</u>tee' (bah<u>ai</u>tei') three
watsewite (watsewiti) four
manegite (manegiti) five
naafaite (naafaiti) six
daatsewite (daatsewiti) seven
nawiwatsewite (nawiwatsewiti) eight
seemonowemihyande (seemonowemihyandi) nine
seemoote (seemooti) ten

Additionally, are these alternative forms:

watsewitee' (watsewitei') four (of something)
manegitee' (manegitei') five (of something)
naafaitee' (naafaitei') six (of something)
daatsewitee' (daatsewitei') seven (of something)
nawiwatsewitee' (nawiwatsewitei') eight (of something)
seemonowemihyandee' (seemonowemihyandei') nine
  (of something)
seemoohtee' (seemoohtei') ten (of something)

The object case forms are given in parentheses. The word for "nine" literally means "one less than ten," and the ending of the number "three"
changes to **bah<u>ai</u>teN** when the postposition **maN** is added to it (refer to
section below).

The numbers 11 through 19 are formed using the phrase **seemoote** [+
number] **man do'<u>ai</u>ngende** ("ten with [number] emerging"). Notice that
the forms for 13 and 19 are irregular.

seemoote semme' man do'<u>ai</u>ngende eleven
seemoote wahatem man do'<u>ai</u>ngende twelve
seemootem bah<u>ai</u>tem man do'<u>ai</u>ngende thirteen
seemoote watsewitem man do'<u>ai</u>ngende fourteen
seemootem manegitem man do'<u>ai</u>ngende fifteen
seemooten naafaitem man do'<u>ai</u>ngende sixteen
seemooten daatsewitem man do'<u>ai</u>ngende seventeen
seemooten nawiwatsewitem man do'<u>ai</u>ngende eighteen
wahaseemonowemihyande nineteen

Notice that the number 19 does not follow the usual pattern and means
"one less than twenty." There is also a shorter version for numbers 11
through 18 which deletes the first word in the phrase, namely, **seemoote**

"ten." For example, number 11 is **semme' man do'a̱ingende** instead of the longer **seemoote semme' man do'a̱ingende**.

Multiples of ten from 10 to 90 are formed by adding the base of each number to the word for 10, **seemoote**, as in **wahaseemoote** "twenty." The object case forms of these numbers are made by replacing the final -e with **-i**. For example, **wahaseemooti**, **baha̱iseemooti**, etc. Here are the Shoshoni numbers from 20 to 100:

wahaseemoote twenty
baha̱iseemoote thirty
watsewiseemoote forty
manegiseemoote fifty
naafaiseemoote sixty
daatsewiseemoote seventy
nawiwatsewiseemoote eighty
seemonowemihyaseemoote ninety
biaseemoote one hundred

Notice that the word for 100 literally means "big ten." The word for 90 literally means "one less than ten times ten." The form for 90 given above is more common with younger speakers; the older (more traditional) way of saying 90 is **seemonowemihyambiaseemoote**.

All of the numbers after three end in the suffix **-te** (or the voiced version: **-de**) in the subject case, and **-ti** in the object case. This particular kind of suffix is known as an "absolutive suffix."

Absolutive suffixes are a class of suffixes that are used on word stems when no other prefixes or suffixes have been added. They are very common in all the Uto-Aztecan languages, take many different shapes, and can occur not only on numbers but also on nouns and adjectives. The stem of the number is what remains after the absolutive suffix has been removed.

Notice that when counting the teens (11–19), the absolutive stem is not removed before adding the postposition **maN** "with" (for example, **wahatem maN**, **baha̱item maN**, etc.), but it is removed before compounding the stem with the word **seemoote** "ten" in order to form the multiples of ten (as in **wahaseemoote**, **baha̱iseemoote**, etc.).

To form the numbers above twenty, use the same formula as for the teens, exept varying the initial word from ten to twenty, to thirty, etc. For example:

wahaseemoote semme' man do'a̱ingende twenty-one
baha̱iseemootem baha̱item man do'a̱ingende thirty-three
biaseemonowemihyande ninety-nine (one less than one hundred)

Multiples of a hundred are formed by adding the stem of the numbers two through nine to the word for "one hundred" (**biaseemoote** "big ten"):

biaseemoote one hundred
wahambiaseemoote two hundred
bahaimbiaseemoote three hundred
watsewimbiaseemoote four hundred
semme'amo'o or **manegimbiaseemoote** five hundred
naafaimbiaseemoote six hundred
daatsewimbiaseemoote seven hundred
nawiwatsewimbiaseemoote eight hundred
(bia)seemooten nam biaseemonowemihyande nine hundred
seemooten nam biaseemoote one thousand

Notice that the word for 500 (**semme'amo'o** "one hand") is irregular. Younger people use the more regular-sounding word **manegimbi-aseemoote**. Also, the word for 1000 literally means "ten times big ten."

DUAL AND PLURAL FORMS OF NOUNS

There are several ways of forming the dual and plural of nouns in Shoshoni. One method is to add suffixes directly to nouns. However, not all nouns can take these suffixes. The dual subject case suffix is **-nehwe**, and the dual object case suffix is **-nehi**.

To put the word **sadee'** ("dog") into the dual, you merely add the dual suffix, using either the subject or object case depending on whether the dual noun is the subject or the object of a verb: **sadee'nehwe** or **sadee'nehi** ("two dogs"). Remember that a glottal stop after a long vowel is usually dropped in pronunciation before the addition of the number suffixes.

The plural subject-case suffix is **-nee'**, and the plural object-case suffix is **-nei'**. To make the word **sadee'** ("dog") plural, add these suffixes depending on which case the noun takes: **sadee'nee'** or **sadee'nei'** ("dogs"). Remember the plural ending is used when meaning three or more. If there are only two, use the dual! The other methods of forming the dual and plural of nouns in Shoshoni will be introduced in later chapters.

DUAL AND PLURAL FORMS OF ADJECTIVES

"True" adjectives are adjectives ending in the suffix **-teN** (object case **-tiN**). True adjectives show number and case by substituting the suffixes **-teN** or **-tiN** for other suffixes.

If an adjective describes two of something, then you can replace **-teN** and **-tiN** with the endings **-tehwe** or **-tehi**, depending on whether the adjective describes something that is the subject (**-tehwe**) or object (**-tehi**) of a verb. The plural endings for adjectives again differ according to case. They are **-tee'** (subject case) or **-tei'** (object case).

Another process used to show duality and plurality is known as "partial reduplication." This involves taking the first syllable of a word, reduplicating it, and prefixing it back onto the word. This method of showing duality can be used by itself and in conjunction with other methods of showing number (such as suffixes). Several adjectives that use partial reduplication are as follows:

>**ohapite**   yellow [singular/subject case]
>**ohapiti**   yellow [singular/object case]
>**o'ohapitehwe**   yellow [dual/subject case]
>**o'ohapitehi**   yellow [dual/object case]
>**o'ohapitee'**   yellow [plural/subject case]
>**o'ohapitei'**   yellow [plural/object case]
>**biaichi'**   big [singular/subject case]
>**biaichi'a**   big [singular/object case]
>**bibiaichinehwe**   big [dual/subject case]
>**bibiaichinehi**   big [dual/object case]
>**bibiaichi'**   big [plural/subject case]
>**bibiaichi'a**   big [plural/object case]

Notice that nominal adjectives (adjectives which are not true adjectives), such as **biaichi'** ("big") and others that do not end in **-teN**, take the same dual and plural endings as nouns (their singular forms take the same case endings as nouns).

In the dual form, the word **biaichi'** takes both a suffix and partial reduplication (**bibiaichinehwe**), while in the plural form of **biaichi'** there is only partial reduplication (**bibiaichi'**).

PLURAL FORMS OF VERBS

Shoshoni verbs do not conjugate in the same way that verbs in English and other related languages do. Suffixes are added to verb roots to show tense (when something happened) and aspect (how something happened). Verbal suffixes (such as **-deN** and **-ku**) are usually the same for all persons, meaning that the suffixes do not change with different subjects, such as first person (I), second person (you), and third person (he, she, or it). However, some Shoshoni verbs do change to show number (whether the subject of the verb is singular, dual, or plural).

There are three classes of verbs that deal with number. Type One verbs indicate the dual form by using the process of partial reduplication. Type One verbs do not show a difference between the singular and plural forms of the verb stem. For example:

> **mi'a-** to walk, go (by foot)
> **ne mi'a'yu** I'm going.
> **nemme mi'a'yu** We [plural/exclusive] are going.
> **mimi'a-** dual form (pronounced: [**miwi'a-**]) (formed by partial
>   reduplication of the first syllable **mi-**)
> **nehwe mimi'a'yu** We [dual/exclusive] are going.

Type Two verbs have one verb root in the singular and a completely different verb root for either the dual, or plural numbers, or both. Examples of Type Two verbs are **habi-** ("to lie") and **gade-** ("to sit"). The dual and plural forms are **gwabi-** ("to lie") and **yegwi-** ("to sit"), respectively. In this lesson you learned the plural verb form **hiwa-** ("to carry, take"), which occurs in the form **hiwange-** (this is actually a causative form) and which has the singular form **yaa-**. This type of root-changing verb is known as a "suppletive verb."

Type Three verbs show no change in the verb stem depending on number, and they have the same verb stem whether the subject is singular, dual, or plural. Fortunately for the learner, the majority of Shoshoni verbs fall within either Type One or Type Three.

COUNTING OBJECTS

When indicating two of anything in Shoshoni, there are two possibilities: (1) use the dual suffix on the noun, or (2) use the dual suffix on the noun with the appropriate form for the number "two." For example:

> **sadee'nehwe** two dogs
> **wahatehwe sadee'nehwe** two dogs

Shoshoni nouns always take the dual and plural endings, even when a number is present, as in **bahaitee' sadee'nee'** ("three dogs"). Remember that the cardinal number and the noun must both agree in number (singular, dual, or plural) and case (subject, object, or possessive) with each other.

ASKING ABOUT PRICES

The verbs **naninakai-** and **nanimee-** mean "to cost." They take the habitual- customary verb suffix (**-deN**) when referring to the price of an object. There are separate words for "dollar" (**wanadeboope**), "quarter" (**dubiichi**), and "fifty cents" (**u sengwaibiN**).

Prices in Shoshoni are given in the formula, [number] **wanadeboope** [coin] **ma'ai**. For example, $1.50 is **semme' wanadeboope, u sengwaibim ma'ai** (literally, one dollar with half of it.)

Vocabulary for Drills

ishe himbaiga naninakaide? How much does this cost?
    himbaiga how much?
    naninakai- to cost
    naninakaide it costs (HABITUAL-CUSTOMARY)
    naninakaite (PAUSAL FORM)
wanadeboope (-ha) dollar
dubiichi (-ha) quarter (twenty-five cents)
u sengwaibim ma'ai with half of it (half a dollar or fifty cents)
    sengwaibiN half (only in reference to money) [N class]
    sengwai'biN (PAUSAL FORM) [N class]
    ma'aiH with (in addition to) [H class]
nanimee- to cost (dialectical variant of **naninakai-**)
    nanimeede it costs (CUSTOMARY-HABITUAL)
    nanimeete (PAUSAL FORM)
seemono ten [adv] (for counting money or age)
manegiseemono fifty [adv] (for counting money or age)
biaseemono hundred [adv] (for counting money or age)
dosa- white [prefixed attributive adjective]
waahni' (waahni'a) fox
bibiaichinehwe (-nehi) big [dual]
ai'aingabitehwe (-tehi) red [dual]

Drill 1. How much do different items cost in Shoshoni?

Q: **Ishe himbaiga naninakaide?**
    A1: **Semme' wanadeboope, naninakaide.**
    A2: **Semme' wanadeboope naninakaide, u sengwaibim ma'ai.**
    A3: **U sengwaibi naninakaide, dubiichi ma'ai.**
    A4: **Seemono nanimeede.**

A5: **Manegiseemono nanimeede.**
A6: **Biaseemono nanimeede.**

DRILL 1, ENGLISH TRANSLATION:

Q: How much is this (pointing to object)?
A1: One dollar. ($1.00)
A2: A dollar fifty. ($1.50)
A3: Seventy-five cents. (75¢)
A4: Ten dollars. ($10.00)
A5: Fifty dollars. ($50.00)
A6: One hundred dollars. ($100.00)

Drill 2. What did you see?

Q: **Hinna enne buiki?**
A1: **Bahaitei' sadee'nei' ne buiki.**
A2: **Watsewitei', dosa-bungunei' ne buiki.**
A3: **Manegitei' daiboo'nei' ne buiki.**
A4: **Naafaitei', waahni'nei', ne buiki.**
A5: **Ne wahatehi, bibiaichinehi, ai'aingabitehi mu'biinehi buiki.**

end of
Tape 3-a

DRILL 2, ENGLISH TRANSLATION:

Q: What did you see (before just now arriving)?
A1: I saw three dogs (and have just arrived).
A2: I saw four white horses (and have just arrived).
A3: I saw five white men (and have just arrived).
A4: I saw six foxes (and have just arrived).
A5: I saw two big, red cars (and have just arrived).

7

Maitengate hagai′ neesungaahka?
("What's it like outside?")

- Talking about the Weather and Seasons of the Year
- Expressing Likes and Dislikes
- Adverbs of Place and Time

Vocabulary for Dialog 1

start of
Tape 4-a

genduN yesterday [adv] [N class]

sikiteN right here [adv] [N class]

dakaweiH- to snow [H class]

    dakáweihwa it snowed (MOMENTANEOUS)

    dakawe′i it snowed (DURATIVE)

    gai dakawe′i it didn't snow (DURATIVE)

wei- to rain

    we′i it rained (DURATIVE)

dommo in the winter [adv]

    do′mmo (PAUSAL FORM)

    egi dommo this winter (literally, now in the winter)

sooN a lot, much, many [adv/quantifier] [N class]

dakabi (-ta) snow

munna′gwa last year [adv]

    munnaa′gwa (PAUSAL FORM)

himbaigaN how much? [N class]

    gai himbaigaN not much

daa one, someone, somebody, something [indefinite pronoun]

    daaN someone's/one's (POSSESSIVE) [N class]

-gu while, when [subordinating verb suffix]

    dakaweigu while it snowed, when it snowed

getaaN very; really [adv] [N class]

basa- to dry up [intr]
　basánnu dried up (COMPLETIVE)
daazaN summer [noun], in the summertime [adv] [N class]
　daa'zaN (PAUSAL FORM)
gutseniH- to heat up, get hot [H class]
　gutsénihka it heats up, it gets hot; it heated up, it got hot (RESULTATIVE ASPECT)
dommo year [noun]; winter (in this dialog referring to the weather)
　do'mmo (PAUSAL FORM)
andapuN differently [adv] [N class]
nahape has become (PERFECTIVE ASPECT)
　naha- to become
　-pe (PERFECTIVE ASPECT) [verbal suff]
beaiN long ago, a long time ago [adv] [N class]
　beaim beeN long ago, a long time ago
　beeN (EMPHATIC PARTICLE)
ezhe'iN- to be cold [intr] [N class]
　ezhe'inniku as cold (as)
　-niku like . . . , as . . . [postpos] (can be added to nouns, pronouns, and verb stems)
　ezhe'inde (it) is cold (HABITUAL-CUSTOMARY)
ade'uka that's because . . . [sing]
　adehwe'uka [dual]
　adee'uka [pl]
saika [object case] of **saideN**
su'ahaibei- to mess up [tr]
　su'ahaibeidee' people who mess things up [pl]
　-deN (the one who does X) [sing] [N class]
　-dehwe (the two who do X) [dual]
　-dee' (the ones who do X) [pl]

Dialog 1

Dennis's maternal grandmother is visiting her sister.
　Grandma: **Gendu ha sikiten dakáweihwa?**
　Aunt: **Gai', gai dakawe'i, we'i da'ga.**
　Grandma: **Egi dommo, damme soon dakabita suwa'i.**
　Aunt: **Haa', munna'gwa, gaihimbaigan dammi daa dakaweigu, damme sogope basánnu.**
　Grandma: **Dazan dease, getaan dammi gutsénihka.**

Aunt: **Egi siden dammen dommo andapun nahape, g<u>ai</u> be<u>ai</u>m bee ezhe'inniku, ezhe'inde.**

Grandma: **Adee'uka daiboo'nee' s<u>ai</u>ka damme sogopeha su'ah<u>ai</u>beidee'.**

Aunt: **Haa'.**

ENGLISH TRANSLATION:

Grandma: Did it snow here yesterday?

Aunt: No, but it rained all day.

Grandma: We need a lot more snow (around here) this winter.

Aunt: Yes, it was very dry last year.

Grandma: And it was so hot during the summer, too.

Aunt: The weather is changing. It doesn't seem to get as cold in the winter as it used to.

Grandma: That's because the white people have messed up the land.

Aunt: Yes.

LITERAL TRANSLATION:

G: Yesterday question-particle this=one=here snowed-(momentaneous)?

A: No, not snowed(durative), rained(durative) only.

G: Now winter, we(pl/inclusive) much snow-(object case) need(durative).

A: Yes, last=year, not-much it snow-while, our(pl/inclusive) land very dried=out-(completive).

G: Summer also, very to=us(pl/inclusive) is=hot-(resultative).

A: Now this=here our(pl/inclusive) winter different has=become-(perfective) not old=days (particle) be=cold-as, is=cold-(habitual).

G: That's=because white=man-(pl) this=one-(object case) our(plural/inclusive) land-(object case) mess=up-(pl).

A: Yes

Vocabulary for Dialog 2

gahte at (used with verbs that indicate no motion)
  memme gahte where you are from, where you are at [pl]
-'i- (indicates periodical repetitive or habitual action) [prefinal verbal suff]
  wei'i- to rain (periodically over time)
  wei'ide it rains (periodically over time) (CUSTOMARY-HABITUAL)
  wei'iite (PAUSAL FORM)
sooseN a lot, much more [N class]

dakadua′ai- to snow a lot, to accumulate (of snow) [intr]
  dakadua′ai′yu it is snowing a lot, the snow is accumulating (PRO-
    GRESSIVE)
ede′iN- to be hot [N class]
  ede′inde it is hot (HABITUAL-CUSTOMARY)
daza summer [noun]; in the summertime [adv]
  daa′za (PAUSAL FORM)
dahwani spring [noun], in the spring time [adv]
  dahwaa′ni (PAUSAL FORM)
aika [object case] of **aideN**
ege- new, young, fresh [adjective pref]
buhihsea- to sprout (of plants), to have new green growth (of
  plants) (literally, to grow green) [intr]
  buhihseagu while/when sprouting, while/when having new
    green growth (of plants)
yebaani fall/autumn [noun], in the fall/autumn [adv]
  yebaa′ni (PAUSAL FORM)
basakwai- to be/become dry [intr]
  basakwai′nna that which is dry, that which has become dry
    [infinitive gerund suffix]
  -′nna [infinitive/gerund subordinating verbal suff]
gutsenihka′ai- to be continuously hot (of the weather) [intr]
  gutsenihka′ai′yu it is continuously hot (PROGRESSIVE)
-baidu at, toward, to [postpos]
nasundeganaaH- to plan (something) [H class]
  nasundeganaahka plan/plans (RESULTATIVE)
wizha ne soto goonikua′ I should go over that way (to there)
  (indicates movement away from speaker and then back in
  direction of speaker)
  wizha should, might [adv]
  soto over that way [demonstrative locative]
  gooni- to make a round trip, go and come back [intr]

Dialog 2

Duffy has met a Shoshoni-speaking man named Mike from Nevada.
They are talking to each other at Idaho State University.
  Duffy: **Memme gahte ha soo wei′ide?**
  Mike: **Gaihimbaiga weide sikite, memme gahte soose we′i.**
  Duffy: **Dommo wihyu?**
  Mike: **Dommo nemme gahte, soon dakadua′ai′yu.**

Duffy: **Daaza wihyu?**

Mike: **Daazan nemme gahte getaa ede'inde.**

Duffy: **Dahwaani wihyu?**

Mike: **Dahwaani nemme gahten tsaan neesungande, aika hinna ege buhihseagu.**

Duffy: **Yebaani wihyu?**

Mike: **Nemme sogope getaan basakwai'nna, dease nemme gahte getaan gutsenihka'ai'yu.**

Duffy: **Ne Nevada-baidu nasundeganaahka, dahwaani wizha ne soton goonikua'.**

ENGLISH TRANSLATION:

Duffy: Does it rain a lot in Nevada?

Mike: Not as much as here.

Duffy: How about in the winter?

Mike: We get a lot of snow in the winter.

Duffy: How about in the summer?

Mike: It's very hot in the summer.

Duffy: How about in the spring?

Mike: It is very beautiful there in the spring because all the plants are green.

Duffy: How about in the fall?

Mike: It's very dry and hot.

Duffy: I think that when I go to Nevada, I'll go in the spring.

LITERAL TRANSLATION:

D: You(pl) at question-particle much rain-do-(habitual)?

M: Not-much rain-(habitual) this=one=here, you(pl) as much-(adverbial) rain(durative)

D: Winter then?

M: Winter we(pl/exclusive) at, much snow-accumulate-(progressive).

D: Summer then?

M: Summer we(pl/exclusive) very is=hot-(habitual).

D: Spring then?

M: Spring we(pl/exclusive) at good it=feels-(habitual), this=one-(object case) thing(object case) new is=green-while.

D: Autumn then?

M: Our(pl/exclusive) land very is=dried=out-while, also we(pl/exclusive) at very is=hot=continuously-(progressive).

D: I Nevada-at plan-(resultative), spring should I to=there(not visible) go=and=come-go=and=do

Language and Culture

TALKING ABOUT YOURSELF AND BEING POLITE

You must be careful when speaking Shoshoni not to talk about yourself too much. Boasting can be considered extremely rude in Shoshoni society, especially when a person is discussing personal likes, dislikes, and abilities. A few basic rules to help avoid any cultural misunderstandings are:

1) It is always more polite to use "we" than "I."

2) Use "I" with close friends and members of your family, in informal situations, and when you are sick or in need of some kind of help.

3) It is impolite to speak for others, especially in repeating others' opinions.

4) Boasting is always considered impolite. The traditional way of honoring someone is to hold a giveaway in his or her honor.

5) It is only appropriate to tell people what you like and dislike when asked directly, but you should never volunteer this kind of information.

6) It is more polite to refer to relatives by their titles (such as "my grandfather" or "my sister") rather than by their given names.

7) Always greet everyone present, whether you know them or not.

Grammar

MORE DEMONSTRATIVE PRONOUNS: **s-** PREFIX;
OBJECT AND POSSESSIVE CASES

The initial prefix **s-** can be used on the demonstrative proximal prefixes **i-, ai-, o-, a-, u-** when they are in combination with the base ending **-teN/-deN** or the adverb of place ending **-ki/-ku.**

For example, from Dialog 1 we have **sikiteN** "right here" (from **ikiteN**) and **saika** "this" (not close enough to touch) (from **aika** [object case] of **aideN**).

The initial prefix **s-** CANNOT be used with the demonstrative proximal prefixes when they occur with the base **-sheN** (**isheN, aisheN, oseN, aseN, useN**). Remember that the base **-sheN** is used when presenting (introducing) something or when contrasting something with something else. The base **-deN**, on the other hand, is used when introducing "new" information into a conversation (i.e., the kind of information that one cannot assume the listener already knows.) The addition of the initial prefix **s-** onto demonstrative pronouns shows that the information it is referring to is "given" (or old) information. Given information in English is most commonly signaled by the definite article "the." For example, in order to say "the cat" (given information) in English, you assume that the listener knows the specific cat. However, if you were to simply say "a cat" (new information), you assume the listener does not have prior knowledge of that particular cat.

A useful rule for when to add the **s-** prefix is to use it in Shoshoni when you would use the definite article "the" in English. Otherwise, listen to how fluent speakers use it, and try to imitate them.

The following shows the demonstrative pronouns with the **-deN** base in three cases:

Subject Case	Object Case	Possessive Case
	Singular	
(s)ideN	(s)ika	(s)ikaN
(s)aideN	(s)aika	(s)aikaN
(s)odeN	(s)oka	(s)okaN
(s)adeN	(s)aka	(s)akaN
(s)udeN	(s)uka	(s)ukaN
	Dual	
(s)idehwe	(s)idehi	(s)ideheN
(s)aidehwe	(s)aidehi	(s)aideheN
(s)odehwe	(s)odehi	(s)odeheN
(s)adehwe	(s)adehi	(s)adeheN
(s)udehwe	(s)udehi	(s)udeheN
madehwe	madehi	madeheN
	Plural	
(s)idee'	(s)idei	(s)ideeN
(s)aidee'	(s)aidei'	(s)aideeN
(s)odee'	(s)odei'	(s)odeeN
(s)adee'	(s)adei'	(s)adeeN
(s)udee'	(s)udei'	(s)udeeN
madee'	madei'	madeeN

ADVERBS OF PLACE AND TIME

The demonstrative distal prefixes **i-, ai-, o-, a-, u-** can be added with or without the **s-** prefix to **-ki/-ku** to form an adverb of place meaning "here" or "there." The base **-ki** is used with **i-** and **ai-**. The base **-ku** is used with **o-, a,-** and **u-**:

(s)iki right here
(s)a̱iki here (not close enough to touch)
(s)oku there
(s)aku over there
(s)uku there (out of sight)

Here are two examples using the above adverbs of place:

Haga' ne gwasu'u? Iki. Where's my dress? Right here.
Ne bia' uku gooninei' ne dawi' ma'i. My mother went there with
   my younger brother.

Adverbs usually do not take any case endings in Shoshoni. This is especially true for adverbs of time. The following are the most common
adverbs of time:

egi daba̱i'yi today
egi now (right now)
gendu yesterday
iwaa' tomorrow
bea̱ichehkuse in the morning
egi bea̱ichehku this morning
gendum bea̱ichehku yesterday morning
iwaa' bea̱ichehku tomorrow morning
yeitaba̱i'yi in the afternoon
egi yeitaba̱i'yi this afternoon
gendu yeitaba̱i'yi yesterday afternoon
iwaa' yeitaba̱i'yi tomorrow afternoon
yeika in the evening
egi yeika this evening
gendu yeika yesterday evening
iwaa' yeika tomorrow evening
dommo in the winter
egi dommo this winter
munna'gwa dommo last winter
egi dommo gimaginde next winter
dahwaani in the spring
egi dahwaani this spring
munna'gwa dahwaani last spring
egi dahwaani gimaginde next spring
daaza in the summer
egi daaza this summer
munna'gwa daaza last summer

egi daa'zan gimaginde next summer
yebaa'ni in the fall
egi yebaa'ni this fall
munna'gwa yebaa'ni last fall
egi yebaa'ni gimaginde next fall

end of
Tape 4-a

ADJECTIVES

Adjectives in Shoshoni have to agree with the noun they describe in both number (singular, dual, or plural) and case (subject, object, or possessive).

Adjectives in Shoshoni are categorized into three groups:

1) Prefixed adjectives are attached to the noun they describe. For example, the prefixed adjective **bia-** means "big," as in **bia'ape'** "father's older brother" (literally, big father).

2) Nominal adjectives are nouns used as adjectives, such as the Shoshoni word for the color "pink": <u>ai</u>nga'<u>ai</u>bi'.

3) True adjectives can end in one of six absolutive suffixes. Shoshoni shares absolutive suffixes with all the other Uto-Aztecan languages. These are suffixes that are added to words (mostly nouns and adjectives) but that no longer have any grammatical function.

Absolutive suffixes are rarely removed from a word, and have predictable (although often irregular) case endings. The six absolutive suffixes used with true adjectives are:

a) **-bite** (**-biti** [object case]); this suffix is used only on color adjectives. For example:

start of
Tape 4-b

> <u>ai</u>ngabite red color
> <u>ai</u>ngabiti red color [object case].

b) **-pe** (**-peha**) The absolutive suffix **-pe** added to a verb changes it to a noun. For example:

> **deka-** to eat [verb]
> **dekape** food [noun]
> **dekapeha** [object case]

The absolutive suffix **-pe** added to a noun changes it to an adjective. For example:

> **yuhu** fat, lard [noun]
> **yuhupe** fat [adj]
> **yuhupeha** fat [adj] [object case]

c) **-deN** (**-di**) For example:

> **gebedande** long [adj]
> **gebedandi** [adj] [object case]. Remember that the absolute suffix **-deN** is different from the customary-habitual aspect suffix on verbs.

d) **-bichi** (**-bichiha/-bichi'a**) For example:

>   **egebichi** new [adj]
> **egebichiha** [adj] [object case].

e) **-tsi'/-chi'** (**-tsi'a/-chi'a**) For example:

> **biaichi'** big [adj]
> **biaichi'a** [adj] [object case]. NOTICE: (1) **biaichi'** is related to the prefixed adjective **bia-** ("big") as in **bia'ape'** ("father's older brother"). (2) The absolute suffix **-tsi'/-chi'** is the same as the diminutive suffix that is used to show feelings of affection on the part of the speaker toward an object, person, or animal, as in **ne biatsi'** ("my dear/little mother").

f) **-be** (**-beha**) For example:

> **beaitembe** old [adj]
> **beaitembeha** [adj] [object case].

THE PARTICIPIAL SUFFIXES -deN AND -pe

The suffixes **-deN** and **-pe** are regularly added to verbs to change them into adjectives and nouns. For example:

> **wahyaN-** to burn [verb]
> **wahyande** fire [noun]
> **nade'asenge-** to be frozen [verb]
> **nade'asengepe** frozen [adj].

The suffixes **-deN** and **-pe** are equivalent to the past participles in English (such as eaten, broken, finished, etc.).

Words formed with the **-deN** suffix share a semantic sense that the action is the normal state of affairs and continual over a period of time. For example, the suffix **-deN** added to the verb **ogwai-** "to flow" (of water) changes it into the adjective "flowing" or the noun "river," "stream": **ogwaideN** "flowing" [adj], **ogwaideN** "river," "stream" [noun], **ogwaiteN** (PAUSAL FORM).

The suffix **-pe** added to a verb gives it the meaning of being the result of prior action of the verb. For example:

deka- to eat
dekape eaten [adj]
dekape food [noun]
dekapeha [object case]
daigwa- to speak
daigwape spoken [adj]
daigwape language, speech, word(s) [noun]
daigwapeha [object case].

PREFINAL VERBAL SUFFIX -'i-

The verbal suffix -'i- can be added directly to a verb stem before any tense/aspect or auxiliary verb suffixes. The verbal suffix -'i- gives the verb the additional meaning of repetitive or habitual action over a period of time. For example, from Dialog 2:

Memme gahte ha soo wei'ide? Does it rain a lot where you're from?
wei- to rain
wei'i- to rain repetitively/a lot.

COORDINATION

Coordination refers to how a language connects phrases together into larger units. The most common connecting words in Shoshoni are

deaseN also, too
wihyu then, and then, what about . . . ?
ma'ai and, together with
da'ga only, just, but

Coordination words regularly follow the word to which they are attached. For example:

da'zan dease also in the summer
da'za wihyu? What about the summer?
em bia' ma'ai with your mother
ne bia' da'ga just/only my mother

Coordination words can also be used to connect whole phrases. The following are examples from the dialogs:

Gendu ha sikiten dakáweihwa? Did it snow here yesterday?
Gai', gai dakawe'i, we'i da'ga. No, it didn't snow, it only rained.
Nemme sogope getaan basakwai'nna, deasen nemme gahte getaan gutsenihka'ai'yu. Our land, which is very dry, also where we live it is very hot.

One coordination word used to form sentences that give reasons and explanations to a question is **ade'uka** (similar to the English coordination "that's because . . . "). This word has a dual form (**adehwe'uka**) and plural form (**adee'uka**). Notice in the example from Dialog 1 the plural form is used, since it refers to **daiboo'nee'** (white people).

Adee'uka daiboo'nee' saika daa sogopeha su'ahaibeidee'.
That's because the white people have messed up the land.

VERBS EXPRESSING LIKES AND DISLIKES

One verb that expresses "to like" in Shoshoni is **tsaasuaN-**:

Ne dakabita tsaasuange'nna. I like the snow. (REPETITIVE ASPECT)

The negative form of this verb is irregular. The negative is not formed with the negative particle **gai** ("not"). The word **deche** is inserted in front of the object that one dislikes, and **tsaa-** in **tsaasua-** is dropped:

Ne deche dakabita suange'nna. I don't like the snow. (REPETITIVE ASPECT)

This formation is very common, especially among younger speakers and children. The pattern is use **tsaaN-** with a verb to indicate liking something, and use **deche** in front of the object that you dislike, along with dropping **tsaaN-** before the verb. The following are some examples using the verb **gesunga-** "to taste":

Ne gapii'a tsaangesunga'. I like coffee. (DURATIVE ASPECT)
Ne deche gapii'a gesunga'. I don't like coffee. (DURATIVE ASPECT)

The more common pattern for adult speakers is to use the verb that fits with the item being described. Thus, to state that you do not like coffee or fry bread, you can simply say

Ne gai gapii'a hibide. I don't drink coffee. (CUSTOMARY-HABITUAL)
Ne gai yuhudegumahannipeha dekade. I don't eat fry bread. (CUSTOMARY-HABITUAL)

INDEPENDENT AND DEPENDENT (RELATIVE) CLAUSES

There are two types of clauses in any language: independent and dependent clauses. Independent clauses express a complete idea by themselves and can stand by themselves. For example, some independent clauses in English are: He makes basketry. She wondered out loud. He slept in late this morning.

Dependent (or relative) clauses do not express a complete idea and cannot stand by themselves. They are part of another clause, which itself is independent. In English, dependent or relative clauses are connected to the main or independent clause by such words as "who," "whom," "which," "that," and "what." For example, some dependent clauses in English are "which she made by herself," "that he had read in the paper," "to whom she owed more than just her current position."

Dependent (or relative) clauses in Shoshoni are formed using special suffixes that are added to the verb. The dialogs in this chapter introduce two subordinating suffixes: **-gu** and **-'nna**.

THE SUBORDINATING VERBAL SUFFIX **-gu**

The suffix **-gu** is added directly to the stem of the verb in the dependent clause. The suffix **-gu** corresponds to the English "when" or "while." The suffix **-gu** is used when the actions of the verbs in both the dependent and independent clauses are simultaneous or nearly simultaneous. For example:

Munna'gwa, ga̲i̲ himba̲i̲gan dammi dakaweigu, damme sogope getaam basánnu. Last year, when it didn't snow very much, our land was very dry.
Ne dekagu, neam bia' awogozhoha̲i̲pe'nni. While I was eating, my mother was washing dishes.

THE INFINITIVE/GERUND SUBORDINATING VERB SUFFIX **-'nna**

The suffix **-'nna** is also used to form dependent or relative clauses; it is added to the stem of the verb of the dependent clause. The time of the action of this verb is taken from the tense of the verb in the independent clause. Clauses with this suffix can be translated using "which," "that," "who," etc. For example:

Nemme sogope getaam basakwai'nna, deasen nemme gahten getaan gutsenihka'a̲i̲'yu. Our land, which is very dry, also where we live, is very hot.
Ide yuhudegumahanipe nean deka'nna, deche gamma'nna. The fry bread, which I am eating, doesn't taste good.

Notice that the dependent clause, **ne deka'nna** ("which I am eating"), is not marked in Shoshoni by a word equivalent to the English "which," "that," "who," etc. The pause after the dependent clause signals to the listener(s) the presence of a dependent clause.

The verb suffixes on both the dependent verb (**deka-**) and the independent verb (**gamma-**) perform completely different functions, even though they look the same.

The suffix **-'nna** on the verb **deka-** is an infinitive/gerund subordinating suffix. A very formal example in proper Shoshoni is

Iden gapii' ne hibi'nna, debizhi getaa ede'i'nna.
The coffee (that) I'm drinking is too hot.

A less formal example of the same thing is

Nean gapii' getaangu gutsénihka. My coffee is too hot.

Notice that the above example uses the verb **gutseniH-** "to be hot."

THE NOMINALIZING SUFFIX **-deN**

The nominalizing suffix **-deN** can be added to the stem of a verb to indicate the person who does the action of the verb. The suffix **-deN** looks the same as the habitual-customary aspect and changes depending on case and number.

-deN	for the singular	**-di**	[object case]
-dehwe	for the dual	**-dehi**	[object case]
-dee'	for the plural	**-dei'**	[object case]

The nominalizing suffix can be added to the verb **neka-** "to dance" to mean "a person who dances" or "a dancer":

nekadeN dancer (**nekadi** [object case])
nekadehwe two dancers (**nekadehi** [object case])
nekadee' dancers (three or more) (**nekadei'**[object case])

Vocabulary for Drills

dabai'wa all day long [adv]
baa'ema- to rain hard (pronounced [baa'ewa-])
 baa'e'ma it rains/rained hard (DURATIVE) (pronounced [baa'ee'wa])
 baa'emafe'nni it is/was raining hard (CONTINUATIVE) (pronounced [baa'ewafe'nni])
baazagaiH- to sprinkle, rain lightly [H class]

baazaga'i it sprinkles/sprinkled (DURATIVE)

baazagaife'nni it is/was sprinkling (CONTINUATIVE)

baagenaiH- to be foggy [H class]

baagenaihka it is/was foggy (RESULTATIVE)

baagenaihka'nna that/while it is foggy [relative clause]

dabaishu'aiH- to be sunny [H class]

dabaishu'ai-gande to have sunshine

dabaishu'aihka it is sunny (RESULTATIVE)

dowoaH- to be cloudy [H class]

dowoahka it is/was cloudy (RESULTATIVE)

neai"- to blow (of wind), be windy [G class]

ne'ai it is/was windy (DURATIVE)

neaipe'nni it is windy (CONTINUATIVE)

neaide it is windy (CUSTOMARY-HABITUAL)

neaite (PAUSAL FORM)

neaidi [object case] of **neaide**

de'ase- to be freezing cold (of weather)

de'aseka it is freezing cold (RESULTATIVE)

maitengahte outside (used with static verbs that indicate no motion)

gwiipusiaH- to be smoky (of the environment) [H class]

gwiipusiahka it is/was smoky (RESULTATIVE)

hukuneaiH- to blow dust [intr] [H class]

hukuneaife'nni it is blowing dust (CONTINUATIVE)

tsaasuaN- to like, think well of [intr] [N class]

tsaasuange'nna likes/like (REPETITIVE)

suaN- to think, want, feel, need [tr] [N class]

deche suaN- to dislike [tr]

deche suange'nna dislikes/dislike (REPETITIVE)

daa weinna that/while it is raining [relative clause]

daam baagenaihka'nna that/while it is foggy [relative clause]

tsaawesunga- to feel good about (something), to like (something)

tsaawesunga' feels/feel good about, likes/like (DURATIVE)

wesunga- to feel (something)

deche wesunga- to dislike, not feel good about

deche wesunga' dislikes/dislike, doesn't/don't feel good about
(DURATIVE)

daan gutsenihka'nna that/while it is hot [relative clause]

wagande with (someone), to, toward (someone) [postpos]

wagandi [object case] of **wagande**

ezhe'ika'nna that/while it is cold [relative clause]

ezhe'indi [object case] of **ezhe'inde**

Drill 1

Answer the following question about how the weather was yesterday:

Q: **Memme gahte, gendu hagai' neesungaahka?**

    A1: **Gendun dab<u>ai</u>'wa, nemme gahten dakáwe'i.**

    A2: **Gendun dab<u>ai</u>'wa, nemme gahte baa'e'ma.**

    A3: **Gendun dab<u>ai</u>'wa, nemme gahte baazaga'i**

    A4: **Gendun dab<u>ai</u>'wa, nemme gahte baagenaihka.**

    A5: **Gendun dab<u>ai</u>shu'ai-gande, getaan nemmi gutsénihka.**

    A6: **Gendun dab<u>ai</u>'wa, nemme gahte dowoahka.**

    A7: **Gendun dab<u>ai</u>'wa, nemme gahte ne'<u>ai</u>.**

    A8: **Gendun dab<u>ai</u>'wa, nemme gahten getaan de'aseka.**

    A9: **Gendun dab<u>ai</u>'wa, nemme gahte hukune'<u>ai</u>.**

    A10: **Gendun dab<u>ai</u>'wa, nemme gahte gwiipusiahka.**

ENGLISH TRANSLATION:

Q: What was the weather like yesterday where you live?

    A1: It snowed all day yesterday.

    A2: It rained hard all day yesterday.

    A3: It sprinkled all day yesterday.

    A4: It was foggy all day yesterday.

    A5: It was hot and sunny all day yesterday.

    A6: It was cloudy all day yesterday.

    A7: It was windy all day yesterday.

    A8: It was freezing cold all day yesterday.

    A9: It was blowing dust all day yesterday.

    A10: It was smoky all day yesterday.

Drill 2

Answer the following question about how the weather is outside:

Q: **Maitengahte hagai' neesungaahka?**

    A1: **Dakáweife'nni.**

    A2: **Baa'emafe'nni.**

    A3: **Baazagaife'nni.**

    A4: **Baagenaihka.**

    A5: **Dab<u>ai</u>shu'aihka.**

    A6: **Dowoahka.**

    A7: **Ne<u>ai</u>pe'nni.**

    A8: **De'aseka.**

    A9: **Hukune<u>ai</u>fe'nni.**

    A10: **Gwiipusiahka.**

ENGLISH TRANSLATION:
Q: What's it (the weather) like outside?
A1: It's snowing.
A2: It's raining hard.
A3: It's sprinkling.
A4: It's foggy.
A5: It's sunny.
A6: It's cloudy.
A7: It's windy.
A8: It's freezing cold.
A9: It's blowing dust.
A10: It's smoky.

Drill 3

Duffy and Dennis are discussing the weather. Whatever Duffy says, Dennis contradicts her by saying just the opposite.

1a: **Ne dakabita tsaasuange'nna.**
   1b: **Ne deche dakabita suange'nna.**
2a: **Daa weinna ne tsaasuange'nna.**
   2b: **Ne deche daa weinna suange'nna.**
3a: **Ne daam baagenaihka'nna tsaasuange'nna.**
   3b: **Ne deche daam baagenaihka'nna suange'nna.**
4a: **Neaidi ne tsaawesunga'.**
   4b: **Ne deche neaidi wesunga'.**
5a: **Ne getaan dammen daan gutsenihka'nna tsaasuange'nna.**
   5b: **Ne getaan dammen daan gutsenihka'nna deche suange'nna.**
6a: **Ne damme wagandi getaa ezhe'ihka'nna tsaasuange'nna.**
   6b: **Ne deche ezhe'indi suange'nna.**

end of
Tape 4-b

ENGLISH TRANSLATION:
1a: I like the snow.
   1b: I hate the snow.
2a: I like the rain.
   2b: I hate the rain.
3a: I like the fog.
   3b: I hate the fog.
4a: I like the wind.
   4b: I hate the wind.
5a: I like the heat.
   5b: I hate the heat.
6a: I like the cold.
   6b: I hate the cold.

8

Beaichehkuse, hinna enna hanni'yu?
("What do you do in the morning?")

- Talking about Daily Routines
- Asking about Jobs and Occupations
- Telling the Time
- Expressing the Time of Day

Vocabulary for Dialog 1

start of
Tape 3-b

naakiH- to become, get to be (in time) [H class]
    naakihka (it) becomes/gets to be (RESULTATIVE)
dammen dabai naafaitenga naakihka at six o'clock in the morning
yeze- to get up; fly [intr]
    yee'ze- (PAUSAL FORM)
    yezemi'i'yu (I) usually get up (on a habitual basis) (PROGRESSIVE
        ASPECT)
    yezemi'ii'yu (PAUSAL FORM)
    -mi'i- [indicates habitual, repeated action] (HABITUAL-ITERATIVE)
        [prefinal verbal suff]
dunaa' then; right away [adv] (see note below)
nagozhohai- to bathe [intr]
    nagozho'hai- (PAUSAL FORM)
    nagozhohaineitsi after (I) have usually gone and bathed
    -nei- to go and [+ verb] (and return) (AUXILIARY VERB)
    -tsi after having [+ verb] [subordinating verbal suff]
nawasoaH- to get dressed [intr] [H class]
    nawasoahwai'nna (I) habitually get dressed
    -kwai'nna/-hwai'nna to habitually [+ verb] (a special form that
        always takes the iterative)
    nawasoa' put on your clothes! (IMPERATIVE)
    nawasoakua' go (and) put on your clothes!

binnagwa   then, later [adv]

   binna'gwa (PAUSAL FORM)

daadekaH-   to eat breakfast [H class]

   daadekahwatsi   after (I) have eaten breakfast

   daadekahwa'tsi (PAUSAL FORM)

   -hwa- (MOMENTANEOUS ASPECT)

dede'ai-   to work

   dede'a'i   work/works (DURATIVE)

   dede'ai'i-   to work (doing something on a daily basis)

nuki-   to run

   dede'ainukimi'i-   to run off to work (on a daily basis)

haga'ahti?   where at?

-gatei'   at; people at (a specific location) [pl] (see note below)

dezateboofoingeH-   to teach [intr] [H class]

   dezateboofoinge'nna   teach/teaches (ITERATIVE ASPECT)

tsateboofoingeH-   to teach (something) [tr] [H class]

   tsateboofoinge'nna   teach/teaches (something) (ITERATIVE ASPECT)

hayangenaa'   first, first thing (see note below)

   ha'yangenaa' (PAUSAL FORM)

dedaigwa-   to read [intr]

   dammen daiboo' dedaigwa'nna   written materials (in English) [nom-
     inalized verb], reading materials (in English) [nominalized verb]

tsateboofoingehwai'nna   (I) teach on a daily basis

yeitabai'yi   in the afternoon [adv]

   yeitabai'yi (PAUSAL FORM)

dammen newedaigwa'nna   speaking (the) Indian (language) [nomi-
  nalized verb]

-tegi-/-degi-   to start, to begin; to be (in a place), be seated; to put
  (AUXILIARY VERB)

   tsateboofoingedegimi'i-   to start teaching (something) on a
     daily basis

himbai'   when?

dabaidekaH-   to eat lunch [H class]

   dabaidekaneimi'i-   to usually go (away) to eat (and then come
     back) (on a habitual basis)

dogwai-dabai'yi   noon, 12 o'clock noon

   dogwai   right (at), exactly [adv]

dabai'yi   noon, at noon [adv]

go'aiH-   to return, go back, come back [H class]

   go'aihki-   to come home (from perspective of speaker)

   go'aihkimi'i-   to usually come home (on a habitual basis)

naafaitenga daa naakihka at six o'clock
su'ana at about, around, usually [adv]

NOTE: **dunaa'**, **-gatei'**, and **hayangenaa'** drop their final glottal when followed by another word in fluent speech. This includes words like **udei'**, and words with the plural endings like **-nee'** or **-nei'**.

Dialog 1

Dennis is visiting his maternal aunt at her house. They are in the living room talking.

Dennis: **Beaichehkuse, hinna enne hanni'i'yu?**

Aunt: **Ne beaichehkuse, dammen dabai naafaitenga naakihka, yezemi'i'yu. Ne dunaa nagozho'haineitsi, nawasoahwai'nna.**

Dennis: **Hinna dease?**

Aunt: **Binna'gwa ne daadekahwatsi, dede'ainukimi'i'yu.**

Dennis: **Haga'ahti ennen dede'aide?**

Aunt: **Ne Sho-Ban High gatei dezateboofoinge'nna.**

Dennis: **Hinna enne udei tsateboofoinge'nna?**

Aunt: **Beaichehkuse, ha'yangenaa, ne dammen daiboo'dedai-gwa'nna udei tsateboofoingehwai'nna, wihyu yeitabai'yi ne dammen newe-daigwa'nna dease udei tsateboofoingedegimi'i'yu.**

Dennis: **Himbai' ennen dabaideka'ai'yu?**

Aunt: **Ne dogwai-dabaiyi, dabaidekaneimi'i'yu.**

Dennis: **Himbai' ennen go'aihkimi'i'yu?**

Aunt: **Su'ana naafaitenga daa naakihka.**

ENGLISH TRANSLATION:

Dennis: What do you do in the morning?

Aunt: I usually get up at six in the morning. Then I take a bath and get dressed.

Dennis: And then what?

Aunt: I eat breakfast and then go to work.

Dennis: Where do you work?

Aunt: I'm a teacher at Sho-Ban High.

Dennis: What do you teach?

Aunt: First thing in the morning I teach reading, and then in the afternoon I teach the Shoshoni language.

Dennis: When do you eat lunch?

Aunt: I go and eat lunch at noon.

Dennis: When do you come home?

Aunt: Usually at six p.m.

LITERAL TRANSLATION:

    D: Early, what(object) you do-usually-(progressive)?

    A: I early, our(pl/inclusive) day six-at becomes-(resultative), get=up-usually-(progressive). I then bathe-did=and=came-after, get=dressed -habitually-(iterative).

    D: What(object) also?

    A: Later I eat=breakfast-(momentaneous)-after, work-run-usually-(progressive).

    D: Where-at you work-(habitual)?

    A: I Sho-Ban High at(pl) teach-(iterative).

    D: What(object) you those=ones(object) teach-(iterative)?

    A: Early, first=of=all, I our(pl/inclusive) white man reading=material those=ones(object) teach-usually-(iterative), then in=the=afternoon I our(pl/inclusive) Indian spoken=material also those=ones(object) teach-start-usually-(progressive).

    D: When you eat=lunch-usually-(progressive)?

    A: I exactly at=noon, eat=lunch-did=and=came-usually-(progressive).

    D: When you return-come-usually-(progressive)?

    A: Around six-at (particle) becomes-(resultative).

Vocabulary for Dialog 2

nemmi us; for us (here: "for my family") [pl, exclusive]
degumahanninge- to cook for (someone)
    degumahaninngebidegwa'ai'yu (I) usually arrive and go cook for (someone) on a habitual basis (PROGRESSIVE)
    -bide- to arrive and [+ verb] (AUXILIARY VERB)
    -gwa- (indicates direction away from the speaker)(AUXILIARY VERB)
-mahwaka after (we) finish [+ verb]-ing (AUXILIARY VERB)
    nemmi dekamahwaka after we [pl, exclusive] finish eating
awogozhohai- to wash dishes
    awogozho'hai- (PAUSAL FORM)
    awogozhohaikwai'nna (I) usually wash the dishes
    awo (awoi') dish, plate
      aa'wo (PAUSAL FORM)
    gozhohai- to wash (something) [tr]
    gozho'hai- (PAUSAL FORM)
subai' then (cf. with **su'bai** "in there")
ducha- dirty [adjective pref]

> **ducha'awo (ducha'awoi')** dirty dishes
>
> **sa͟itu** over here [adv]
>
> **dahna-** to set down (something)
>
>> **nadahnakandu'i** will be set down (PASSIVE FUTURE)
>>
>> **nadahna-** to be set down (PASSIVE)
>>
>> **na-** [passive verb pref]
>
> **sesewe'** sometimes
>
> **dezakeena-** to sew (something) (transitive verb)
>
>> **ne dezakeena'a͟i'yu** I'm usually working on my beadwork (literally, sewing) (PROGRESSIVE)
>
> **noondea** or else, otherwise
>
> **dembui-** to watch
>
>> **dembuitegi'i'yu** (I) usually sit and watch (PROGRESSIVE)
>>
>> **dembuitegi'ii'yu** (PAUSAL FORM)
>>
>> **dembuitegi-** to sit and watch
>>
>> **-tegi-** to be seated; begin, start; put
>
> **habi-** to lie down [intr]
>
>> **ha'bi-** (PAUSAL FORM)
>>
>> **habikwai'nna** (you) go to bed (ITERATIVE ASPECT)
>
> **dugu** must, have to [adv]

Dialog 2

Dennis continues to ask his maternal aunt about her daily routine.

> Dennis: **Hinna enne hanni'i'yu, go'a͟ihwatsi?**
>
> Aunt: **Ne nemmi degumahanningebidegwa'a͟i'yu. Nemmi dekamahwaka, ne dunaa awogozho'ha͟ikwai'nna.**
>
> Dennis: **Hagani'yunde?**
>
> Aunt: **Suba͟i' nemmen ducha'awo ga͟i soo sa͟itu nadahnakandu'i. Ne gizhaa suka suange'nna.**
>
> Dennis: **Hinna ennen dease hanni'i'yu?**
>
> Aunt: **Sesewe' ne dezakeena'a͟i'yu, noondea television-ha dembuitegi'i'yu.**
>
> Dennis: **Himba͟i' enne habikwai'nna?**
>
> Aunt: **Su'ana seemootenga, ne habikwai'nna.**
>
> Dennis: **Neam bia' dugu tsaam bennen ga͟i dede'aide.**

ENGLISH TRANSLATION:

> Dennis: What do you do when you get home?
>
> Aunt: First of all, I make dinner for my family. After we eat, I wash the dishes immediately.

Dennis: Why?

Aunt: Because I don't like a lot of dirty dishes everywhere.

Dennis: And then what do you do?

Aunt: Sometimes I work on my beadwork, and sometimes I just watch TV.

Dennis: What time do you usually go to bed?

Aunt: I usually go to bed at ten o'clock.

Dennis: I'm glad my mother doesn't have to go to work.

LITERAL TRANSLATION:

D: What(object) you do-usually-(progressive), return-(momentaneous)-after?

A: I us(pl/exclusive) cook=for-arrive-(direction-away-from-speaker)-usually-(progressive). us(pl/exclusive) eat-after=finishing, I then dishes-(object) wash-usually-(iterative).

D: Why?

A: then our(pl/exclusive) dirty=dishes not much over=here (passive)-set=down-(future). I not=good (definite)-that=one-(object) feel-(repetitive).

D: What(object) you also do-usually-(progressive)?

A: Sometimes I sew-usually-(progressive), otherwise television-(object) watch-sit usually-(progressive).

D: When you lie=down-usually-(iterative)?

A: Around ten-at, I lie=down-usually-(iterative).

D: My mother must good self not work-(habitual).

Language and Culture

ORTHOGRAPHIES

An "orthography" is the writing system of a language. Three major types of writing systems are in use today. The first type of writing system uses an alphabet. In this system, used in English and Shoshoni, each character represents a particular sound or several sounds in the language. A second type of writing system uses a syllabary, where each character represents a complete syllable of the language. Syllabaries are very common throughout the world, and in the Western Hemisphere they are used for writing languages such as Cherokee, Cree, and Inuit. A few languages, such as Chinese, still use orthographies based on pictographs and logographs, where each character is an iconic (pictorial) representation of either an object (pictograph) or an abstract idea (logograph).

ORTHOGRAPHY AND IDEOLOGY

The orthography of a language is often the result of a conscious decision by speakers of the language. The orthographic system of a particular language may be the result of political, ethnic, and religious influences. For example, Serbs and Croats in Europe speak virtually the same language; however, Croats are generally Catholic and write their language with the Roman alphabet, while Serbs mostly belong to the Serbian Orthodox Church and write their language with the Cyrillic alphabet (the same alphabet as that used for the Russian language with some minor changes).

Sometimes the official writing system of a language reflects the dialect of people in power at the time of its adoption. For example, the English writing system reflects how words were pronounced in the London area around 1472 when the spelling was first "fixed" by the Printers' Guild of London under the direction of William Caxton. The English language since that time has borrowed many words from other languages (mainly French, Latin, and Greek) and, for the most part, has kept the same spelling as in the original languages.

Often the writing system of a particular language will reflect dialectal differences. For example, in Shoshoni there is no one dialect that is considered more prestigious or the "standard form." This is the case for many nonstate languages (i.e., they are not the "official" language of a political entity) and therefore have no natural center of power to initiate standardization.

The same language can have more than one orthography. For example, even though English spelling has been standardized since 1472, there are several different ways of spelling the same word. In America we write that the "tires" of our car hit the "curb"; in England they write that the "tyres" of their car hit the "kerb." There are multiple ways of spelling the same word in English because more than one government or center of power uses English, and each government makes its own rules concerning how the language should be spoken and written.

SHOSHONI ORTHOGRAPHIES

There are many dialects of Shoshoni. Since no single dialect of Shoshoni is considered to be more prestigious than any other, all of the writing systems adopted by Shoshoni speakers tend to reflect their specific dialects. The orthography of the Shoshoni language used here is only one of several currently used to represent the language. Two other orthographies used in a number of Shoshoni publications are:

1) The Tidzump Orthography, which reflects the Eastern Shoshoni dialect of Wind River, Wyoming.

2) The Miller Orthography, which reflects the Goshute and Western Shoshoni dialects from eastern Nevada and western Utah.

THE MILLER ORTHOGRAPHY

The main differences between the Miller orthography and the ISU system used in this course are the ways the Shoshoni consonantal sounds are represented.

The following is a comparison of the differences in how the two systems represent the Shoshoni consonants. The Miller orthography uses the following nineteen letters (which may be used either as a single letter or as a combination of two letters): **a, ai, e, h, i, k, kw, m, n, o, p , s, t, ts, u, w, y,** and **'**. The vowels have the same value in both the Miller orthography and the ISU orthography. Long vowels are indicated by doubled vowels, and doubled **ai** and **ai** are written **aai** and **aai** in the Miller system.

The first class of sounds are called the "stop" consonants. The pronunciation of stop consonants involves completely blocking or momentarily stopping the flow of air out of the mouth. The following is a comparison of the two systems:

ISU Orthography	Miller Orthography
b-	p-
-b-	-p-
d-	t-
-d-	-t-
g-	k-
-g-	-k-
gw-	kw-
-gw-	-kw-
-k-	-kk-
-kw-	-kkw-
-p-	-pp-
-t-	-tt

Notice that the hyphens indicate where vowels may occur.

Here is a summary first of the ISU orthography, followed by a description of the differences in the Miller orthography.

The Idaho State University system represents "stop" consonants at the beginning of a word with **b, d,** and **g**. When the hard sounds, **b, d,** and **g**, occur within a word between two vowels, the ISU system represents them as **p, t,** and **k**.

The soft versions of these three sounds (which can occur only between vowels) are represented in our system as **b, d,** and **g**. When two words are combined to form a compound word, if the first letter of the second word is **b, d,** or **g** and takes the soft sound when combined, then the two words will be written as one. For example, **newe** "Indian" and **daigwape** "language" combine to become **newedaigwape** "Indian language," and the **d** in **daigwape** now takes on the soft sound. If, however, when two words are combined, the first sound in the second word retains its hard sound, then a hyphen will be inserted between the two words to indicate that the second word has kept the hard sound. For example, **soo** "many" and **gahni** "houses" combine to form the name **Soo-gahni** "Blackfoot (Idaho)," and the **g** in **gahni** keeps the hard sound.

In the Miller orthography these same sounds at the beginning of a word are represented as **p, t,** and **k**. The hard sounds within a word (between two vowels) are written doubled as in **pp, tt,** and **kk**. The soft sounds within a word (between two vowels) are written **p, t,** and **k**.

The nasal sounds (produced when air escapes through the nose) **m** and **n** are identical in both orthographies except that the ISU system uses a single **m** and **n** between vowels that take the soft sounds of **w** and **y**.

The semivowels **w** and **y** are represented the same way in both systems.

The glottal sounds (produced in the back of your throat) **h** and **'** (the glottal stop) are represented the same way in both systems, although the glottal stop is not always represented in the Miller orthography.

The sibilants (or hissing sounds) are the sounds **s** and **ts**. In the Miller orthography the letter **s** can represent either **s** or **sh** in the ISU system. In the Miller orthography if **s** is preceded by either **i** or **ai**, then it represents the **sh** sound.

ISU Orthography	Miller Orthography
s-	s-
except for	
-sh-	-is-
-sh-	-ais-

The consonant sound **ts** in the Miller orthography can represent **ts, z,** and **zh** in the ISU orthography. The sound **ts** at the beginning of a word in the Miller orthography is equivalent to **ts** in the ISU system. When **ts** occurs between two vowels within a word in the Miller orthography, it can be pronounced either **z** or **zh**. If **ts** is preceded by either **i** or **ai**, it will be pronounced **zh**, otherwise it is pronounced as **z**.

ISU Orthography	Miller Orthography
ts-	ts-
-z-	-s-

except for

ISU Orthography	Miller Orthography
-zh-	-its-
-zh-	-<u>ai</u>ts-

In the Miller orthography all consonants can occur in four different forms: (1) simple form; (2) prenasalized (with an **n** preceding); (3) geminated (or doubled); or (4) preaspirated (with an **h** preceding). The following lists all of the consonants that occur in the Miller orthography with the prenasalizing **n**:

ISU Orthography	Miller Orthography
-nn-	-nn-
-mm-	-mm-
-mb-/-mp-	-mp-
-nd-	-nt-
-ng-	-nk-
-ngw-	-nkw-
-ndz-/-nts-	-nts-

The following lists all of the geminated (doubled) consonants in the Miller orthography as compared to the ISU system:

ISU Orthography	Miller Orthography
-p-	-pp-
-t-	-tt-
-k-	-kk-
-kw-	-kkw-
-ts-	-tts-

except for

ISU Orthography	Miller Orthography
-ch-	-itts-
-ch-	-<u>ai</u>tts-

The following lists all of the preaspirated consonants (with an **h** preceding) in the Miller orthography as compared to the ISU system:

ISU Orthography	Miller Orthography
-f-	-hp-
-ht-	-ht-
-hk-	-hk-
-hw-/-hkw-	-hkw-

-hs-	-hs-
-hw-/-hm-	-hm-
-hn-/-hy-	-hn-
-hy-	-hy-
-hw-	-hw-

The Miller orthography represents the three final features as **-N** (silent **n**), **-H** (preaspirating feature), and **-"** (geminating feature). There are also a number of words in the Miller orthography that end in a small-case **h**. The vowel directly preceding this **h** is always devoiced (whispered). For example, **tekkappeh [dekape]** "food."

EXAMPLE WORDS IN THE ISU AND MILLER ORTHOGRAPHIES

The following list of example words in both orthographies are the same words that appeared in Chapter 1; their meanings can be found there:

ISU Orthography	Miller Orthography
ada'	ata'
ha	ha
baa'	paa'
haa'	haa'
ege-	eke-
enne	enne
neesungaahka	neesunkaahka
sadee'	satee'
nammi'	nammi'
siipungu/sii-bungu	siippunku
biidennu	piitennu
dogo'	toko'
mo'	mo'
gotoo'	kottoo'
gotoonoo'	kottoonnoo'
u	u
yuhu	yuhu
yuuta'	yuutta'
duutaiboo'/duu-daiboo'	tuuttaipoo'
b<u>ai</u>de'	p<u>ai</u>te'
g<u>ai</u>'	k<u>ai</u>'
daiboo'	taipoo'
hainji	haintsi
dease	tease

ISU Orthography	Miller Orthography
mea'	mea'
dei'	tei'
bia'	pia'
newezoiga'i	newetsoika'i
dua'	tua'
bui	pui
sogope	sokoppeh*
mase	mase
natesu'	nattesu'
<u>ai</u>kwehibite	<u>ai</u>kkwehipitteh*
baa'	paa'
bazi'	patsi'
babi'	papi'
sohoo'bi	sohoo'pi
saa'b<u>ai</u>	saa'p<u>ai</u>
huchuu'	huittsuu'
be<u>ai</u>chehku	pe<u>ai</u>ttsehku
guchu	kuittsu
deheya'	teheya'
dosabite	tosapitteh*
ada'	ata'
doyadaiboo'	toyataipoo'
gaa'	kaa'
gap<u>ai</u>	kapp<u>ai</u>
daga'	taka'
basigoo'	pasikoo'
haga'	haka'
ohapite	ohappitteh*
hainji	haintsi
iki	ikki
duka	tukka
duku	tukku
m<u>ai</u>ku	m<u>ai</u>kku
be<u>ai</u>chehkuse	pe<u>ai</u>ttsehkuse
mu'bii	mu'pii
muu'bi	muu'pi
mia'	mia'
damme	tamme
dommo	tommo
memme	memme

ISU Orthography	Miller Orthography
naniha	naniha
gedii'	ketii'
Dzoon	Tsoon
naafaite	naahpaitteh*
dakáweife'nni	takkaweihpenni
nawa'aipe'	nawa'aippe'
banabui'	pannapuiH
enne	enne
bannaite'	pannaitte'
hi'nna	hinna
gahni	kahni
guhnáiki	kuhnaikki
bungu	punku
baingwi	painkwi
wenangwa	wennankwa
siipungu/sii-bungu	siippunku
tso'ape	tso'appeh*
ape'	appe'
sosoni'	sosonni'
buhihseagu	puhihseaku
ishe	ise
gaishe	kaise
nazatewa'	natsattewa'
yuuta'	yuutta'
himbaigandengahtu	himpaikantenkahtu
tsaa'	tsaa'
tsadamani	tsatammanni
tsiina'	tsiinna'
wongoo'bi	wonkoo'pi
wenangwa	wennankwa
waapi	waappi
dowoahka	tomoahka
nee'we	nee'we
dawi'	tami'
nehwe	nehwe
dahwe	tahwe
yamba	yampa
guyungwi'yaa'	kuyunkwi'yaa'
gaiyu'	kaiyu'
wihyu	wihnu

ISU Orthography	Miller Orthography
dapaihyaa'	tappaihyaa'
bazi'	patsi'
nazatewa'	natsattewa'
gizhaa'	kitsaa'
dai'zhi	tai'tsi
bia'ape'	pia'appe'
ba'i	pa'i
a'aa'	a'aa'
da'oo'	ta'oo'
gadenoo'	katennoo'
bia'	pia'
haa'	haa'
nemme ape'	nemme appe'
nemmen daga'	nemmen taka'
nemmen nammi'	nemmen nammi'
nemmen tsiina'	nemmen tsiinna'
nemmen genu'	nemmen kennu'
nemmem bia'	nemmem pia'
nemmem mu'bii	nemmem mu'pii
deheya'	teheya'
dehe'ya	tehe'ya
mu'bii	mu'pii
muu'bi	muu'pi
daga'	taka'
da'ga	ta'ka
no'yo	no'yo
noo'yo	noo'yo
yuhudegumahanipe	yuhutekumahannippeh*

* Words with an asterisk end in a voiceless vowel, which is signaled by a word final **h** in the Miller orthography.

Grammar

DIRECTIONAL VERB SUFFIXES: **-ki-, -kuaN-, -nei-**

The Shoshoni language has a number of verbal suffixes that are attached directly after the verb root to show direction, known as the "directional verb suffixes." These suffixes determine whether the action of the verb is going away from or coming toward the speaker, or whether the speaker left to perform the action and then returned.

The suffix **-ki-** shows direction toward the speaker. For example, in Dialog 1 of this lesson we have the verb **go'aiH-** "to return" and the verb **go'aihki-** "to return coming in the direction of the speaker."

The suffix **-kuaN-** shows direction away from the speaker, to go and do "x," as in the sentence **ne dekákuandu'i**, "I'm going to go eat." The suffix **-kuaN-** here shows that the speaker is going to go somewhere away from where he or she is at the present time to eat. (Note that this suffix may also be pronounced **-guaN-** by some speakers).

The suffix **-nei-** indicates that the subject went somewhere to perform the action of the verb and then returned. For example, the verb **dabaidekanei-** indicates to go (somewhere) and eat lunch (and then return). Do not confuse the suffix **-nei-** with the tense/aspect suffix **-nei'**, which is added directly to the verb root to show that someone or something has gone and done the action of the verb and now returned.

SHOWING HABITUALITY AND THE VERBAL SUFFIXES -'i-, -ai-, -mi'i-

The Shoshoni language is very concerned with describing precisely how the action of a verb occurs, occurred, or will be occurring. For example, the suffix **-deN** shows habitual or continual action.

In this lesson you have been introduced to three verbal suffixes that are also used to indicate that the action of a verb occurs on a habitual (in most cases daily) basis. The three suffixes are **-'i-, -'ai-, -mi'i-**. Each suffix is attached directly onto the verb root before the addition of any tense/aspect suffixes, and they are generally interchangeable but cannot co-occur with one another.

AUXILIARY VERBS

You have also met four new auxiliary verbs in this lesson: **-tegi-, -kwai-, -nuki-,** and **-bide-**.

The auxiliary verb **-tegi-** means "to begin (to)," "to start (to)," "to place or set," or "to be seated and [+ verb]." It can also be directly attached to the verb stem. For example, **tsateboofoingetegimi'i-** "to usually start teaching."

The auxiliary verb **-kwai-** has a number of meanings in Shoshoni depending on what verb and tense/aspect suffixes are used with it. For example, **-kwai-** is used with the iterative aspect to mean "usually" or "habitually," as in **awogozho'haikwai'nna** "usually washes the dishes."

The verbs **nuki-** "to run" and **bide-** "to arrive" can be added to a verb stem to mean either "to run and [+ verb]" or "to arrive and

[+ verb]." For example, **dede'ainuki-** "to run off to work" and **deguma-hanningebide-** "to arrive and cook for."

THE UNSPECIFIED OBJECT PREFIX **de-**

The prefix **de-** is commonly used and usually means "unspecified object" or "something." It is used to make transitive verbs intransitive. For example, the verb **tsateboofoingeH-** "to teach (something)" is transitive (takes a direct object). To make this verb intransitive (no direct object is necessary), you add the unspecified object prefix to get **dezate-boofoingeH-** "to teach."

The addition of the prefix **de-** to a verb stem can sometimes change the meaning unpredictably as in the following examples: **deka-** "to eat," **dedeka-** "to steal," **da̱igwa-** "to speak," **ded̲aigwa-** "to read," **bui-** "to see," **dembui-** "to watch." Notice that even though **de-** does not end in the prenasaling final feature (or silent **n**), it is pronounced with the prenasaling final feature in **dembui-**.

HOW TO SAY "AFTER [VERB]-ING" AND "AFTER [VERB]-ED"

A subordinating verbal suffix is used in Shoshoni to express "after [+verb]-ing" and "after [verb]-ed." The suffix introduced in this lesson is **-tsi**, and is added onto the verb after any tense/aspect suffixes. This suffix is very useful when describing a series of actions that have occurred one after the other. The dialogs in this lesson use the suffix three times.

In Dialog 1 Dennis's aunt says, **Ne dunaa nagozho'ha̱ineitsi, nawa-soahwai'nna** (literally, "I then, after having gone and bathed and come back, get dressed"). The suffix **-tsi** follows the auxiliary verbal suffix **-nei-**, and indicates that the action of bathing preceded the action of getting dressed.

Also in Dialog 1 Dennis's aunt says, **Binna'gwa ne daadekahwatsi, dede'ainukimi'i'yu** (literally, "Later after I ate breakfast, (I) regularly run off to work"). Here the suffix **-tsi** follows the momentaneous aspect suffix **-hwa** showing that the action of eating breakfast was quickly completed before the action of running off to work took place.

In Dialog 2 Dennis asks, **Hinna enne hanni'i'yu, go'a̱ihwatsi?** (literally, "What do you usually do after (you) returned?") Here, again, the suffix **-tsi** follows the momentaneous aspect suffix **-hwa**. Even though the verb **go'a̱ihwatsi** comes second in the sentence, the suffix **-tsi** tells the listener(s) that the action of the verb (returning) actually precedes the action of the first verb (usually do) in real time.

TELLING THE TIME

Traditionally, Shoshoni people used the position of the sun to determine the time of day. Today, of course, Shoshoni people use clocks and watches like everyone else, and their language has had to develop ways of describing the time according to the hours on the face of the clock.

Normally, Shoshoni people only refer to the hours when telling the time in Shoshoni (such as one o'clock, two o'clock, etc.), and normally do not give more exact times using minutes past or to the hour (such as five minutes to three, six thirty etc.). If you need to be more exact in stating the time, you can always use English. Remember that many Indian people do not have the same slavish need to run their lives according to the clock, as is common in Anglo-American society (this has often been humorously referred to as "Indian time" by both Indian people and non-Indian people alike).

To ask someone the time, you say, **Hinga dab<u>ai</u> nahaa'yu?** (literally, "what (time of) day is it becoming?"). The same verb (**nahaa'yu**) is also used in answering this question. Shoshoni distinguishes between A.M. and P.M. If it is P.M., then you just say the time (such as one o'clock, two o'clock, etc.), but if it is A.M., then you begin the time with the word **be<u>ai</u>chehku** (literally, "morning").

To describe the hours in Shoshoni, use the following pattern:

[number] + **dab<u>ai</u>n goonipe nahaa'yu**. For the numbers two through eight, and ten, use the following forms of the numbers:

wahan two
bah<u>ai</u>n three
watsewin four
manegin five
naafain six
daatsewin seven
nawiwatsewin eight
seemonon ten

For example, two o'clock P.M. is **wahan dab<u>ai</u>n goonipe nahaa'yu**, and two o'clock A.M. is the same with the addition of the word for morning: **be<u>ai</u>chehku, wahan dab<u>ai</u>n goonipe nahaa'yu**. The final word (**nahaa'yu**) is often omitted, as in **wahan dab<u>ai</u>n goonipe** (two o'clock P.M.)

The Shoshoni forms for one o'clock, nine o'clock, eleven o'clock, and twelve o'clock are slightly different. One o'clock A.M. is **dogw<u>ai</u> duga'ni do'<u>ai</u>wha, semme' ga nahaa'yu** (literally, "emerged (from) midnight, it's becoming one"). One o'clock P.M. is **semme'an dab<u>ai</u>n goonipe ga**

nahaa'yu. Notice this is similar to the regular pattern discussed above, with the addition of the possessive case ending on **semme'** "one," and the postposition **ga** added before the verb **nahaa'yu**. Similar to one o'-clock above, Shoshoni nine o'clock also involves the addition of the pos-sessive case ending to the number: **seemonowemihyan dabain goonipe (nahaa'yu)**. In order to distinguish A.M. from P.M. you simply add the word **beaichehku** "morning" at the beginning in the usual way. Eleven o'clock A.M. is expressed as **dogwai-dabai'yiti wepite, sewen dabain goonipe**. Eleven o'clock P.M. is expressed as **dogwai duga'nita wepite, sewen dabai goonipe**. Noon is expressed as **dogwai dabai'yi** (literally, "half of the day"); midnight is expressed as **dogwai duga'ni** (literally, "half of the night").

NOMINALIZED VERBS

In this lesson you have been introduced to many terms for occupations. Most of these nouns are formed from verbs with particular suffixes added (not always tense/aspect suffixes). One common suffix added to verb stems to turn the word into a noun meaning "someone who . . . " is **-gwapi**. You have already encountered the following words using this suffix in this lesson:

> **dezahannigwapi** driver
> **denihannigwapi** judge, lawyer
> **deboogwapi** writer, journalist, secretary
> **nadewagagwapi** cashier, vendor, merchant
> **dedaposi'igwapi** carpenter
> **denito'aigwapi** singer
> **witua-wepa'igwapi** drummer

Vocabulary for Drills

> **dede'a'i** work/works (DURATIVE of **dede'ai-**)
> **deaipede (-i)** child
> > **dedeaipedee' (-dei')** children [pl]
> **newedaigwape (-ha)** the Indian people's language
> **gahyunde** at
> **tsateboofo'i** teach/teaches (DURATIVE of **tsateboofoiN-**)
> **dedakooni' (-a)** policeman
> > **natesu'ungahni (natesu'ungahni)** hospital
> **natesu'uN (-na)** medicine [N class]

deka-gahni (-gahni) restaurant

nadeweengahni (nadeweengahni) store

gunawaimungu (gunawaimungi) train, boxcar; railroad

dede'aingeH- to work for (someone/something) (CAUSATIVE form
of **dede'ai-**) [H class]

　dede'ainge'nna work/works for (ITERATIVE)

　daiboo'nei' dede'ainge'nna (he) works for the white men

　newi dede'aingehka (he) works for the (Shoshone-Bannock)
　tribes (RESULTATIVE)

dewaseange- to farm [intr]

　ne dewaseange'i'yu I farm (on a habitual basis) (PROGRESSIVE AS-
　PECT)

　maseange- to plant, sow, raise (animals) [tr]

　mase'a plant/plants, sow/sows, raise/raises (DURATIVE)

bozheena (bozheenai) buffalo, bison

　bozhee'na (bozhee'nai) (PAUSAL FORM)

dezahanni- to drive (a vehicle)

　dezahannigwapi (-ha) driver (of a vehicle)

denihanni- to judge (someone/something) [tr]

　denihannigwapi (-ha) judge/lawyer

deboo- to write, to draw [tr]

　deboogwapi (-ha) writer; journalist; secretary

nadewaga- to sell

　nadewagagwapi (-ha) cashier, vendor, merchant

dedaposi'igwapi (-ha) carpenter

denito'ai- to sing [intr]

　denito'aigwapi (-ha) singer

witua' (wituai') drum; pot

wepa'i- to slap, to hit

　witua-wepa'igwapi (-ha) drummer

deboofoi- to study

　ne deboofoide I (habitually) study (CUSTOMARY-HABITUAL), I am a
　student

　ne deboofoite (PAUSAL FORM)

hinga dabai what time (of day)?

　hinga dabai nahaa'yu? what time (of day) is it?

do'aiH- to emerge, to come out, to go out, to go upward [H class]

　do'aihwa emerged, came out (MOMENTANEOUS)

dogwai duga'ni do'aihwa semme' ga nahaa'yu it's one o'clock A.M.

beaichehku morning, in the morning; here: A.M. [numeral]

　dabain goonipe (nahaa'yu) it's [numeral] o'clock

gooni- to make a circle, cycle
goonipe cycled; gone (around) in a circle (PERFECT ASPECT)
dogwai just right, exact(ly) [adv]
dogwai dabai'yi noon, 12 P.M.
dogwai duga'ni midnight, 12 A.M.

Drill 1

Answer the following question

Q: **Hinna ennen dede'a'i?**

A1: **Ne Sho-Ban High gahti, dedeaipedei' tsateboofoinge'nna.**

A2: **Ne dammen newedaigwapeha, ISU gahyunde, tsatéboofo'i.**

A3: **Ne dedakooni'.**

A4: **Ne natesu'ungahni gahti dede'aide.**

A5: **Ne dekagahni gahti dede'aide.**

A6: **Ne naadeweengahni gahti dede'aide.**

A7: **Ne gunawaimungu daiboo'nei' dede'ainge'nna.**

A8: **Ne FMC gahti dede'aide.**

A9: **Ne newi dede'aingehka.**

A10: **Ne dewaseange'ii'yu.**

A11: **Ne guchuna maseangende.**

A12: **Ne bungunei' maseange'ii'yu.**

A13: **Bozheenai ne mase'a.**

A14: **Ne udeen dezahannigwapi.**

A15: **Ne denihannigwapi.**

A16: **Ne udeen deboogwapi.**

A17: **Ne udeen nadewagagwapi.**

A18: **Ne udeen dedaposi'igwapi.**

A19: **Ne udeen denito'aigwapi.**

A20: **Ne udeen witua-wepa'igwapi.**

A21: **Ne gai dede'aide, ne deboofoide.**

ENGLISH TRANSLATION:

Q: What kind of work do you do?

A1: I'm a teacher at Sho-Ban High (tribally run high school at Fort Hall).

A2: I teach the Shoshoni language at ISU.

A3: I'm a policeman.

A4: I work at the hospital.

A5: I work at a restaurant.

A6: I work at a store.

A7: I work for the railroad.

A8: I work at FMC (Food and Machinery Corporation) (former business located on reservation).

A9: I work for the tribes (Shoshone-Bannock tribal government).

A10: I'm a farmer.

A11: I raise cattle.

A12: I raise horses.

A13: I raise buffalo.

A14: I'm a bus driver.

A15: I'm a lawyer/judge.

A16: I'm a secretary/writer/journalist.

A17: I'm a cashier/vendor.

A18: I'm a carpenter.

A19: I'm a singer.

A20: I'm a powwow drummer.

A21: I don't work, I'm a student.

Drill 2

Answer the following question

Q: **Hinga dabai nahaa'yu?**

A1: **Dogwai duga'ni do'aihwa, semme' ga nahaa'yu.**

A2: **Semme'an dabain goonipe ga nahaa'yu.**

A3: **Beaichehku, wahan dabain goonipe nahaa'yu.**

A4: **Wahan dabain goonipe (nahaa'yu).**

A5: **Beaichehku, bahain dabain goonipe (nahaa'yu).**

A6: **Bahain dabain goonipe (nahaa'yu).**

A7: **Beaichehku, watsewin dabain goonipe (nahaa'yu).**

A8: **Watsewin dabain goonipe (nahaa'yu).**

A9: **Beaichehku, manegi dabain goonipe (nahaa'yu).**

A10: **Manegin dabain goonipe (nahaa'yu).**

A11: **Beaichehku, naafain dabain goonipe (nahaa'yu).**

A12: **Naafain dabain goonipe (nahaa'yu).**

A13: **Beaichehku, daatsewin dabain goonipe (nahaa'yu).**

A14: **Daatsewin dabain goonipe (nahaa'yu).**

A15: **Beaichehku, nawiwatsewin dabain goonipe (nahaa'yu).**

A16: **Nawiwatsewin dabain goonipe (nahaa'yu).**

A17: **Beaichehku, seemonowemihyan dabain goonipe (nahaa'yu).**

A18: **Seemonowemihyan dabain goonipe (nahaa'yu).**

A19: **Beaichekhu seemonon dabain goonipe (nahaa'yu).**

A20: **Seemonon dabain goonipe (nahaa'yu).**

end of
Tape 3-b

A21: **Dogw<u>ai</u>-dab<u>ai</u>'yiti wepite, sewen dab<u>ain</u> goonipe.**
A22: **Dogw<u>ai</u> duga'nita wepite, sewen dab<u>ai</u> goonipe.**
A23: **Dogw<u>ai</u> dab<u>ai</u>'yi.**
A24: **Dogw<u>ai</u> duga'ni.**

ENGLISH TRANSLATION:

   Q: What time is it?

      A1: It's one o'clock A.M.
      A2: It's one o'clock P.M.
      A3: It's two o'clock A.M.
      A4: It's two o'clock P.M.
      A5: It's three o'clock A.M.
      A6: It's three o'clock P.M.
      A7: It's four o'clock A.M.
      A8: It's four o'clock P.M.
      A9: It's five o'clock A.M.
      A10: It's five o'clock P.M.
      A11: It's six o'clock A.M.
      A12: It's six o'clock P.M.
      A13: It's seven o'clock A.M.
      A14: It's seven o'clock P.M.
      A15: It's eight o'clock A.M.
      A16: It's eight o'clock P.M.
      A17: It's nine o'clock A.M.
      A18: It's nine o'clock P.M.
      A19: It's ten o'clock A.M.
      A20: It's ten o'clock P.M.
      A21: It's eleven o'clock A.M.
      A22: It's eleven o'clock P.M.
      A23: It's noon.
      A24: It's midnight.

9

Hagapundu sikihyunde?
("Where do I go from here?")

Simple Readings in Shoshoni

This lesson is different from the others. In this lesson we will study some texts in Shoshoni, which will give you practice in reading and will increase your vocabulary. We will also give you some tips on how to continue your studies of the Shoshoni language and culture. In this chapter we only give you the new vocabulary words with an English translation. See if you can break up the individual words into their literal translations yourself.

BABIZHII'

> Babizhii' sogope duka naakande.
> Babizhii'an duku deinde'.
> Babizhii' tsaa sogope ga ba'andi hoo'dade.
> Babizhii' tsaa waziide.

The weasel lives beneath the ground.
The weasel is a very small animal.
The weasel likes to dig holes in the ground with his paws.
The weasel is very good at concealing himself from his predators.

Vocabulary:
   babizhii' (-a) weasel
   naakaN- to live, exist [N class]
   deinde' small, little [adj]
   hoda- to dig
      hoo'da- (PAUSAL FORM)
   sogope (-ha) land, ground, earth
   wazi- to hide [intr/tr]
      waazi- (PAUSAL FORM)

145

HA'NII'

Ha'nii' sogo ba'a, deasem baa' ga naakande.
Ha'nii' getaan dede'aide, tsaan bahaabiden dease.

The Beaver lives both in the water and on the land.
The beaver is a hard worker, and he is also a very good swimmer.

Vocabulary:
ha'nii' (-a) beaver
sogo ba'a on the ground/land
   sogo = sogope
bahaabi- to swim

BUHNI'ATSI

Buhni'atsi sohoobin dukai naakande.
Buhni'atsi nade'eyan nasu'wainde.
Buhni'atsi duibichi'.
Buhni'atsiham bishupe deche gwanaade.

The skunk lives under the trees.
The skunk is very shy.
The skunk is also very handsome (literally, a handsome young man)
The skunk's perfume smells very unpleasant.

Vocabulary:
buhni'atsi (-ha) skunk
nade'eyan nasu'wainde am/is/are very shy (CUSTOMARY-HABITUAL)
   nade'eyaN strong(ly) [adj/adv], strength [noun] [N class]
   nasu'waiN- to be shy [intr] [N class]
duibichi' (-a) (handsome) young man
bishupe (-ha) fart, flatulence, intestinal gas (here: skunk's perfume).
deche bad(ly), unpleasant(ly) [adj/adv]
gwanaa"- to smell [intr]
   deche gwanaade it smells bad/unpleasant (CUSTOMARY-HABITUAL)

MUMBICHI

Mumbichi dugani da'ga, gai nanangahkande yeezegwa'aide.
Soondeem mumbichineem bibiaichi'a buihkandee'.
Mumbichi beem bambi nanna'afundu ha'nnikii'yu.
Sesewe' mumbichi sogope ba'a weneede, sehedukubichi wa'i
   nabuinde.

The owl flies in the night.
The owl makes no noise when he flies away.
Many owls have large eyes.
The owl moves its head in different directions.
Sometimes when the owl is standing on the ground, he looks like a
  bobcat.

Vocabulary:
mumbichi (-ha) owl
nanangahkande is heard [passive, stative]
  nangaH- to hear [H class]
  nanangah- to be heard [passive]
  na- [passive] (verbal pref)
  -kandeN [stative] (used to show no motion in verb) (verbal suff)
    [N class]
yezegwa'ai- to usually fly (away from speaker) [tr]
  yeze- to fly [intr], get up [intr]
  -gwa- = **-kuaN**
  -'ai- [indicates habitual, repeated action]
soondeN (soondi) much, many [N class]
  soondehwe (soondehi) much, many [dual]
  soondee' (soondei') much, many [pl]
soondeem mumbichinee' many owls [pl]
  soondeem mumbichineeN many owls' [pl, possessive case]
gandee' (gandei') to have [pl]
  gande (gandi) to have [sing]
  gandehwe (gandehi) to have [dual]
mumbichi beem bambi the owl's head
  beeN its own [possessive case]
  bambi (bambi) head
nanna'afundu in different ways/directions [adv]
ha'nnikii- to happen, make something happen (here: make move)
  hannikii'yu (it) moves (here: its head) (PROGRESSIVE)
sehedukubichi (-ha) bobcat
wa'i nabuinde look/looks like
  wa'iH like (something) [conj, postpos] [H class]

NE HINNI? (1)

Ne Hinni?
Nean naingi bibiaichi'
Ne tsaan denangande.
Daazan, neam bambipe ondembite, dease yu'naindee'.
Ne dabai'wa wazika'ai'yu.
Wihyu dabai ya'ihwaka, ne bahodeyaigimi'i'yu.
Buhipe, nean tsaa-dekape.
Izhape' neai tsaan gesungande.
Sesewe', ne bungu wa'aihku getaan nukigwai'ii'yu, gai deyai-suande.
Huu-baga wa'i, nean nanambuipe daka gaba nabuinde.
Suden tsitsugahka, bennai ne nukigi'nna.
Dommo, neam bambipe dosabi naakwai'nna.
Ne hinni?
Ga'mmu.

Who am I?
My ears are very big.
I hear very well.
In the summer my hair is soft and brown.
I hide during the day.
When the sun goes down I am hungry.
My favorite food is grass.
Coyotes think I will taste good.
Sometimes I must run as fast as a horse because I don't want to die.
In the snow my footprints look like an arrow.
They point toward the place where I came from.
In the winter my hair becomes white.
Who am I?
Jackrabbit.

Vocabulary:
    naingi (-ha) ear
    tsaan denanga- to hear well [intr]
        denanga- to hear [intr]
    bambipe (-ha) (head) hair
    yu'naindee' (yu'naindei') soft [adj] [pl]
        yu'nainde (yu'naindi) soft [adj] [sing]
        yu'naindehwe (yu'naindehi) soft [adj] [dual]
    wazika'ai'yu (it) usually hides/is hiding (PROGRESSIVE ASPECT)
        wazika- to hide (oneself), be hidden [intr]

wazika'<u>ai</u>- to usually hide (oneself), usually be hidden [intr]

dab<u>ai</u> (dab<u>ai</u>) sun, day, daytime, clock, watch

ya'ihwaka (it) goes down (here: of sun) (RESULTATIVE) (literally, it enters [its home below the earth]) [intr]

    ya'iH- to enter, go in [intr] [H class]

bahodeyaigimi'i'yu (it) usually becomes very hungry

    bahodeyai- to be very hungry, be starving

    -gi- [direction toward the speaker]

    -mi'i- [indicates habitual, repeated action]

buhipe (-ha) (green) grass

tsaa-dekape (-ha) favorite food

izhape' (-a) coyote

bungu wa'<u>ai</u>hku like a horse [adj phrase]

    wa'<u>ai</u>H = wa'iH [H class]

nukigwai'i'yu (it) usually runs very fast (PROGRESSIVE ASPECT)

    nukigwai'ii'yu (PAUSAL FORM)

    nukigwai'i- to run fast (with random movement)

    -gwai- [indicates quick random movement] [prefinal verbal suff]

    -'i- [indicates habitual, repeated action]

deyai-suande want/wants to die

    deyai- to die

    -suaN- to want (to) (AUXILIARY VERB) [N class]

huu-baga (-na) arrow

nanambuipe (-ha) footprint(s)

daka gaba through the snow, in the snow

    daka gaa'ba (PAUSAL FORM)

    daka = dakabi

    gaba through, between, among [postpos]

tsitsugahka (it) points (toward) (RESULTATIVE ASPECT)

    tsitsugaH- to point to, point out [tr] [H class]

    tsi"- with a pointed object [instrumental pref]

bennai from oneself (indicates movement)

    bennaN oneself, self [N class]

    -i [postpositional adjunct] (see Chapter 5)

nukigi'nna that (it) runs (toward the speaker) [subordinating verbal suff]

    nukigi- to run (toward the speaker)

dosabi naakwai'nna which becomes white [subordinating verbal suff]

    naakwai- to become

    dosabi = dosabite

ga'mmu (-i) jackrabbit

NE HINNI? (2)

Ne hinni?
Neam muu'bin gebedande, dease getande.
Tsaandi duhubitin ne godokon gande.
Ne watsewitei' daseweeki' ba'i.
"X"-wa'i, nean daseweeki' nabuinde.
Aani', nean tsaa-dekape.
Ne soon dedotadawengende sohoobin gaa'ba, dease gahni ma.
Semme sohoo'bin gupa, nean dudua'neen gahni.
Sesewe', newe deche ne<u>ai</u> suange'nna.
Nea hubia' "Kekekekeke" m<u>ai</u>. Bia-nanangande.
Dahwani, nean dehimbeha, ne witu-wepa'<u>a</u>inge'nna, sohobi ma.
Ne yezekuahka, nean gasa ohapitenni nabuinde.
Ne hinni?
Wobindotadagi'

Who am I?
My nose is very long and hard.
I wear a beautiful black necklace.
My feet have four toes.
Each foot looks like an "X."
Ants are my favorite food.
I make many holes in trees and in houses too.
My babies' home is inside one of them.
Sometimes people don't like me very much.
"Kekekekeke" is my loud song.
In the springtime I drum on trees for my sweetheart.
My wings look orange when I fly.
Who am I?
Northern flicker.

Vocabulary:

getande (getandi) hard [adj] [sing]
godokoN (-na) necklace [N class]
daseweeki' (-a) toe(s)
aaniN (-na) ant(s) [N class]
dedotadawengeN- to cause many holes (in something) [intr] [N class]
sohoobin gaba through trees, in trees
    sohobin gaa'ba (PAUSAL FORM)
gahni ma on a house, in a house (something visible) [pronounced:
  gahni wa]

sohobin gupa in(side of) a tree, in(side) trees
dudua'nee' (-nei') babies
ne<u>ai</u> me [object case]
   newe deche ne<u>ai</u> suange'nna people don't like me (REPETITIVE ASPECT)
hubia' (hubi<u>ai</u>) song, music
bia-nanangande (it) is loud, (it) sounds loud (CUSTOMARY-HABITUAL)
   bia- big [adj pref]
dehimbe (-ha) sweetheart
witu-wepa'<u>ai</u>N- to drum [intr] [N class]
   witu-wepa'<u>ai</u>ngenna drum/drums repeatedly (REPETITIVE ASPECT)
yezekuaH- to fly away (from the speaker) [H class]
   yezekuahka (it) flies away (from the speaker) (RESULTATIVE ASPECT)
gasa (gas<u>ai</u>) wing
ohapitenni nabuinde (it) looks yellow (PASSIVE, CUSTOMARY-HABITUAL)
   -ni nabuinde to look (like something) [intr] (PASSIVE, CUSTOMARY-HABITUAL) (this form can be used with colors and other adjectives)
wobindotadagi' (-a) northern flicker
   wobindotandagi' (-a) (alternate form)

DAMMEN DUKU

Dammen goo'b<u>ai</u> dammem bambi wenangwa hannihkande.
Damme so'o deasen dammen goob<u>ai</u> ma hannihkande.
Dammem bui deasen dammem bambi ma hannihkande.
Damme wahatehi bui ba'i, dammem bambi ma.
Dammem budusii' dammem bui ba'a hannihkande.
Deasen dammem ga'imbehe ba'an dammen ga'i ma hannihkande.
Dammem mubishipe, dammem muu'bin gupa.
Dammem muubi hoih, dammen goo'b<u>ai</u>, deasen dammen goo'b<u>ai</u> ba'an dammen bambi.
Dammem muubindadawenna dammem muu'bin gupa.
Dammem muubindadawennam bennai dammem mubishipeham hannihkimi'inna?
Dammen n<u>ai</u>ngi man deasen bambi seakande.
Dammen n<u>ai</u>ngi bemma dammen denangahka'nna.
Dammem bambi dammen do'yo ba'an gadeede.
Damme huuku, dammen doo'yon dukai hannihkande.
Dammen tsoapehan gewaga hannihkande damme huuku.
Dammem bihin dammen aawa gupa hannihkande.
Damme soo'wo b<u>ai</u>hyugi dammem bihi, damme aawa gupa.

Damma watseena gewaga dammem gwah<u>ai</u>ntsuhni, dease damme watse dukaihgi dammen nenape.

Dammem bihi getaan dede'aide, dammem beepita s<u>ai</u>tun dammen duku gabai hannifei'ide.

Dammen go'h<u>ai</u>, damme sape gupa.

Dammen dagipoo', deasen damme sape gupa.

Dammen deihgo'h<u>ai</u>, damme sape gupai hannihkande.

Sunni'yunde wihyu g<u>ai</u> dammen duku ga'bai nahaade, bendun dammen dekapeha, gwidape nakwainna.

Our face is on the front of our head.
We have cheeks which are also on our face.
Our eyes are also on our head.
We have two eyes on our head.
Our eyelashes are just above our eyes.
Our eyebrows are on our forehead.
There is snot in our nose.
Our nose is in the middle of our face.
Our nostrils are inside our nose.
Is this where snot passes through?
We have hair growing from the top of our ears.
The ears hear sounds.
Our head sits atop our neck.
Our collarbone is located beneath our neck.
Our collarbone is right next to our shoulders.
Our heart is inside our thoracic cavity.
Next to our liver is our heart, all inside the chest cavity.
Our spine is connected to our rib cage.
And our rib cage is just under the chest.
Our heart pumps blood all throughout our body through veins.
We have large and small intestines and kidneys inside us.
Our food passes through the digestive system and then ends up being feces.

Vocabulary:
duku (dukui) body, flesh
goob<u>ai</u> (goob<u>ai</u>) face
   goo'b<u>ai</u> (PAUSAL FORM)
buiH (-ha) eye(s) [H class]
bambi (bambi) head, hair

hannihkande is/are situated (STATIVE, CUSTOMARY-HABITUAL)
   hannihkaN- to be situated/located (STATIVE)
so'o (so'i) cheek(s)
budusii' (-a) eyelash(es)
ga'imbehe (ga'imbehi) eyebrow(s)
ga'i (ga'i) forehead
mubishipe (-ha) snot, nasal mucus
hoih around [postpos]
   dammem muu'bi hoih around our nose
muubindadawennaN (-na) nostrils [pl] [N class]
   muubindainde (-di) nostril [sing]
hannihkimi'inna (it) happens habitually (ITERATIVE)
   hannihkii- to happen, make happen
   -mi'i- [indicates habitual or repeated action]
seakande (it) grows (STATIVE, CUSTOMARY-HABITUAL)
   seakaN- to grow [intr] (STATIVE) [N class]
   sea"- to grow [tr/intr]
dammen naingi bemma with our ears
   bemma with (instrumental use) [postpos]
denangahka'nna which hears, that hears (STATIVE)
   denangahka- to hear (STATIVE) [intr]
do'yoN (-na) neck [N class]
   doo'yoN (PAUSAL FORM)
huukuN (-na) collar-bone [N class]
tsoape (-ha) shoulder(s)
bihiN (bihiN) heart [N class]
awaN (-na) rib cage [N class]
   aa'wa (PAUSAL FORM)
sowoN (-na) lung(s) [N class]
   soo'woN (PAUSAL FORM)
watseN (-na) rib(s) [N class]
gwahaintsuhni (gwahaintsuhni) spine, backbone
   tsuhni (tsuhni) bone
damme watse dukaihgi under our ribs
   dukaihgi under, below (alternate form of **dukai**)
nenape (-ha) chest, chest cavity
beepi (-ta) blood
gabai through(out) (alternate form of **gaba**)
   dammen duku gabai throughout our body
hannifei'ide (it) pumps fast habitually [tr] (CUSTOMARY-HABITUAL)

      hannifei'i- to pump fast [tr] habitually/repeatedly
      hannifei- to pump fast [tr]
  go'hai (go'hai) intestines
  sape (-ha) stomach
  dagipoo' (-a) kidney
  deihgo'hai (deihgo'hai) small intestine
  gupai (alternate form of **gupa**)
  gwidape (-ha) feces, shit
  benduN through (it) [postpos] [N class]
  naha'ai'yu (it) usually makes/does/becomes (PROGRESSIVE ASPECT)
    naha'ai- to usually make/do/become

FURTHER STUDY OF THE SHOSHONI LANGUAGE

Now that you have made it this far, we hope you will continue your study of the Shoshoni language. In this section, we will give you a few hints on how to continue.

You have now acquired a basic foundation in the language. At this point you may consider buying a formal grammar of the Shoshoni language. Although these are written for linguists and other specialists, you should be able to understand most if not all of the grammar with your basic knowledge of the language. A grammar will also be helpful in answering your questions as they arise in the future.

The most important thing to do at this point is increase your vocabulary in the language. This can be done in one of two ways. If you have access to Shoshoni speakers, try to use Shoshoni as much as possible with them. If there is a word you do not know in Shoshoni, ask the native speakers what the word is. A good idea is to always carry a small notebook with you in which you can note down any new words or phrases you hear. Once you have learned a new word, try using it as much as possible. This will help you in memorizing it.

If you do not have access to Shoshoni speakers, the other possibility is to read texts in the language. This will not only increase your vocabulary but will also introduce you to new grammatical structures. The more you read, the more you will understand. Remember that what may seem difficult at first, will become much easier the more you are exposed to it (through either reading or hearing the language).

Another point to keep in mind is the skill in understanding a language is very different from being able to speak a language. Many people, including many Shoshoni people, can understand a language, but are unable to speak it. In order to improve your speaking skills, you need to use the language as much as possible. If you know Shoshoni speakers, use the language with them as much as possible. If you do not know anyone who speaks Shoshoni, start by saying things to yourself. For example, as you go through your daily routines, describe in Shoshoni (out loud!) what you are doing.

One final point: don't become discouraged. Learning a language is a long-term process. It is better to spend a short period of time every day working on the language than a much longer period of time only once or twice a week. The more often you use the language, the easier it will become.

A LIST OF SOURCES ON SHOSHONI HISTORY, CULTURE, AND LANGUAGE

There are a number of works already published on Shoshoni language and culture. The following is a list of the most accessible works on Shoshoni history:

1. *Handbook of North American Indians,* Vol. 11, *Great Basin.* Warren L. D'Azevedo, editor. Washington, D.C.: Smithsonian Institution, 1986. (This is the most complete work on Great Basin Indians. It includes several chapters on different groups of Shoshoni, Numic languages, Great Basin religion and verbal arts, etc. Perhaps its greatest asset is the very detailed bibliography at the end of the book.)

2. *The Northern Shoshone.* Brigham Madsen. Caldwell, Idaho: Caxton Printers, 1980. (This is the most complete history of the Northern Shoshoni in print, although it can be rather dry reading in places. Madsen uses a wealth of historical information from local newspapers, diaries, journals, and government documents. May be hard to find, but most libraries have a copy of it.)

3. *The Lemhi: Sacajawea's People.* Brigham Madsen. Caldwell, Idaho: Caxton Printers, 1979. (This is a short, readable history of the Lemhi band of Northern Shoshoni, from which Sacajawea came. Although the people live on the Fort Hall Reservation today, they still have maintained their own identity among Northern Shoshoni. This work may be hard to find, although most libraries should have a copy of it.)

4. *The Road on Which We Came / Po'i Pentun Tammen Kimmappeh: A History of the Western Shoshone.* Steven J. Crum. Salt Lake City: University of Utah Press, 1994. (This is a detailed history of the Nevada Shoshoni, written by a member of the Duck Valley Reservation.)

5. *The Shoshonis: Sentinels of the Rockies.* Virginia C. Trenholm and Maurine Carley. Norman: University of Oklahoma Press, 1964. (This is a history of the Eastern Shoshoni, with lots of information about Chief Washakie, leader of the Eastern Shoshoni at the time of the treaty councils in the 1860s.)

The following is a list of works on Shoshoni culture:

1. *Northern Shoshone.* Robert Lowie. AMS Press. (This is a reprint of Lowie's famous 1909 ethnography of the Northern Shoshoni, focusing particularly on the Lemhi. This is a very interesting work from a historical point of view, since many of the cultural practices that Lowie describes are no longer extant among the Northern Shoshoni.)

2. *Shoshone Ghost Dance Religion: Poetry Songs and Great Basin Context (Music in American Life).* Judith Vander. Urbana-Champaign, Illinois: University of Illinois Press, 1997. (Vander is an ethnomusicologist who has been working with the Eastern Shoshoni for many years. This book deals with Shoshoni religion, poetry, and music, and how all three come together in the Ghost Dance.)

3. *The Shoshoni-Crow Sun Dance.* Civilization of the American Indian, Vol. 170. Fred Voget. Norman: University of Oklahoma Press, 1984. (This is a detailed history of the Sun Dance, and how it came to the Shoshoni people.)

4. *The Sun Dance Religion: Power for the Powerless.* Joseph G. Jorgensen. Chicago: University of Chicago Press, 1972. (This is a very interesting study of the Sun Dance religion among the Shoshoni and Ute. There is quite a bit of information about the Fort Hall Shoshoni in this work.)

5. *Shoshone Tales.* Collected by Anna M. Smith, assisted by Alden Hayes. Salt Lake City: University of Utah Press, 1993. (This is a delightful collection of traditional Shoshoni myths in English.)

6. *Newe Hupia: Shoshoni Poetry Songs with CD.* Beverly Crum. Logan, Utah: Utah State University Press, 2002. (This book deals with Shoshoni poetry found in the Ghost Dance songs, written by one of the leading native Shoshoni linguists.)

The following is a list of works on Shoshoni Language:

1. *Western Shoshoni Grammar.* Occasional Papers and Monographs in Cultural Anthropology and Linguistics, Vol. 1. Beverly Crum and Jon P. Dayley. Boise, Idaho: Boise State University, Department of Anthropology, 1993. (This is a very detailed and well-organized grammar of the Duck Valley dialect of Shoshoni, written by a native speaker/linguist (Crum) and a linguist (Dayley). The work, which uses the Miller orthog-

raphy, also contains three fully analyzed texts and a Shoshoni-English glossary.)

2. *Shoshoni Texts.* Occasional Papers and Monographs in Cultural Anthropology and Linguistics, Vol. 2. Beverly Crum and Jon P. Dayley. Boise, Idaho: Boise State University, Department of Anthropology, 1997. (This book contains six Shoshoni texts, with English translation and a full analysis of each text, plus a complete Shoshoni-English glossary of all the words in the texts. The work is written in the Miller orthography.)

3. *Newe Natekwinnappeh: Shoshoni Stories and Dictionary.* Wick R. Miller. Salt Lake City: University of Utah Press, 1972. (This is a collection of Western Shoshoni texts principally in the Gosiute dialect of Shoshoni. This work also contains a short description of Shoshoni grammar, and a Shoshoni-English glossary of all the words in the texts. There is no analysis of the texts, only an English translation. The work, of course, is written in the Miller orthography.)

Sosoni' – Daiboo'an daigwape ma'ai
Shoshoni - English Glossary

(Numbers in parentheses refer to chapters in which the word appears in the vocabulary or is discussed.)

a'aa' (-a) (1) Crow Indian
aani (9) ant(s)
aapo' (-a) (4) apple
ada' (-a) (3) mother's brother (uncle), male cousin, sister's son/daughter [male speech]
adee' (7) they, those (over there) [pl, subject case]
adehi (7) them, those (over there) [dual, object case]
adeeN (7) their (over there) [pl, possessive case]
adeheN (7) their (over there) [dual, possessive case]
adehwe (7) they, those (over there) [dual, subject case]
adeN (3)/(7) that (over there) [sing, subject case]
ade'uka (7) that's because . . . [sing]
adee'uka (7) that's bercause . . . [pl]
agai' (agai') (4) salmon
aka (7) that (over there) [sing, object case]
akaN (7) that (over there) [sing, possessive case]
aku (7) over there [adv of place]
andapuN (7) differently [adv]
ape' (-a) (2)/(3) father
aseN (3) that (over there) (contrastive) [sing, subject case]
a['|waN (-na) (9) rib(s), rib cage
a['|wo (awoi') (8) dish, plate
awogozho['|ha̲i̲- (8) to wash dishes
    (ne) awogozho['|ha̲i̲kwai'nna (7) (I) usually wash the dishes (ITER-
      ATIVE) see also gozho['|ha̲i̲-
a̲i̲'a̲i̲ngabitehwe (-tehi) (6) red [dual]
a̲i̲behibite (a̲i̲behibiti) (5) blue
a̲i̲dee' (7) they, these (not close enough to touch) [pl, subject case]

aideeN (7) their (not close enough to touch) [pl, possessive case]

aideheN (7) their (not close enough to touch) [dual, possessive case]

aidehi (7) they; these (not close enough to touch) [dual, object case]

aidehwe (7) these (not close enough to touch) [dual, subject case]

aidei' (7) they, these (not close enough to touch) [pl, object case]

aideN (3)/(7) this (not close enough to touch) [sing, subject case]

aika (7) this (not close enough to touch) [sing, object case]

aikaN (7) this (not close enough to touch) [sing, possessive case]

aiki (7) here (not close enough to touch) [adv of place]

aikwehibite (aikwehibiti) (5) purple

ainga- (5) red (pref)

ainga'aibi' (-ti/-ta) (5) pink

aingabite (aingabiti) (5) red

aisheN (2) this (not close enough to touch) (contrastive) [sing, subject case]

aisheN (4) thank you

aishimbite (aishimbiti) (5) grey

baa' (bai') (4) water

baa'ema- [baa'ewa-] (7) to rain hard

    baa'e'ma [baa'e'wa] (7) it rains/rained hard (DURATIVE)

    baa'emafe'nni [baa'ewafe'nni] (7) it is/was raining hard (CONTINU-ATIVE)

baagenaiH- (7) to be foggy

    baagenaihka (7) it is/was foggy (RESULTATIVE)

    baagenaihka'nna (7) that it is foggy, while it is foggy [relative clause]

ba'a (5) on top of [postpos]

ba'ande (3)/(5) above, (high) over (static transitive verbs with no motion) [postpos]

ba'angu (5) on top of (transitive verbs of motion; movement toward) [postpos]

baazagaiH- (7) to sprinkle, rain lightly

    baazagaife'nni (7) it is/was sprinkling (CONTINUATIVE)

    baazaga'i (7) it sprinkles/sprinkled (DURATIVE)

babi' (-a) (3) older brother

bahaabi- (9) to swim

bahambia' (-a) (3) brother's wife, sister-in-law [female speech]

baha' (-a) (3) aunt (father's sister), father's female cousin ,brother's son or daughter [female speech]

bahodeyai- (9) to be dying of hunger, be very hungry, be starving [intr]

ba'i (4) to have

ba̱ide' (-a) (3) daughter (also: **ba̱ide** [**ba̱idi**])

-ba̱idu (7) at, toward, to (also: **-ba̱itu**) [postpo]

ba̱ihyugi (5) next to, beside [postpos]

ba̱ingwi (ba̱ingwi) (1) fish

ba̱isheN (5) already

-ba̱itu (see **-ba̱idu**)

baki'ehe' (-a) (2) Blackfoot (Indian)

bambi (bambi) (9) head, hair

bambipe (-ha), (9) head hair

banabui' (-a) (3) window

    banabuiH (-ha) (alternate dialectal form)

bannaite' (-a) (2) Bannock (Indian)

basa- (7) to dry up [intr]

    basánnu (7) dried up (COMPLETIVE)

basakwai- (7) to be dry, become dry [intr]

    basakwai'nna (7) that becomes dry, which becomes dry [relative
      clause]

basigoo' (basigoo'a) (4) Indian potatoes (camas root)

bazi' (-a) (3)/(5) older sister, older female cousin

bea̱ichehku (2) (early) morning

bea̱ichehkuseN (5) (early) in the morning [adv]

bea̱im beeN (7) long ago, a long time ago [adv]

bea̱iN (7) long ago, a long time ago [adv]

bea̱itembe (-ha) (7) old

beepi (-ta) (9) blood

bennaN (9) self (myself, oneself, etc.)

benneN (2) self (myself, oneself, etc.)

bia- big [adj pref]

bia' (-a) (2)/(3) mother, aunt (mother's sister)

bia'ape' (-a) (3) father's older brother

biaguchu (-na) (2) buffalo

biagwasu'u (-na) (5) coat

bia̱ichi' (-a) (6) big

    bibia̱ichinehwe (-nehi) big [dual]

    bibia̱ichi' (-a) big [pl]

bia-nanangande (9) (it) is loud, (it) sounds loud

biaseemote (6) (one) hundred

-bide- (8) to arrive and [+ verb] (AUXILIARY VERB)

bide- (2) to arrive [intr]

    biide- (PAUSAL FORM)

    bidennu (2) has/have arrived, has/have come (COMPLETIVE)

bihiN (bihiN) (9) heart
biiyaiH- (6) to be left over
   biiyaihka (6) is/are left over (RESULTATIVE)
binna[']gwa (8) then, later [adv]
binnagwaseN (2) later [adv]
binnangwa (5) behind (facing speaker) [postpos]
bishupe (-ha) (9) fart, flatulence, intestinal gas, skunk's perfume
bituseN (5) back [adv]
bizhi'yuhu (bizhi'yuhi) (6) butter
bizhi' (-a) (6) udder (of cow), breast, milk
bizhi'guchuN (-na) (6) milk cow (female)
Bohogoi' (2) Gibson (district on the Fort Hall reservation)
Botoode (2) Fort Hall (used by older speakers)
boyokami'a- (2) to trot (of horses), walk [intr] [male speech]
   boyokami'a is/are trotting, is/are walking (DURATIVE) [male speech]
bozhe[']na (bozhe[']nai) (8) buffalo/bison
budusii' (-a) (9) eyelash(es)
buhibite (buhibiti) (5) green
buhidekape (-ha) (6) (head of) lettuce, salad
buhihsea- (7) to sprout (of plants), to have new green growth (literally
   to grow green) [intr]
   buhihseagu (7) while/when sprouting, while/when having new
      green growth (of plants) [relative clause]
buhipe (-ha) (9) (green) grass
buhni'atsi (-ha) (9) (also **bohni'atsi**) skunk
bui- (2) to see [intr/tr]
   buiki (5) saw (something) and just arrived
   buinuhi (2) will see (EXPECTIVE)
bungu (bungui/bungi) (4) horse
bu[']ni- (5) to see by chance, happen to see [tr]
   bu[']nni (5) saw by chance, happened to see (DURATIVE)

daa (7) one, someone, somebody, something [indefinite pronoun]
daadekaH- (8) to eat breakfast
   daadekahwatsi (8) after having eaten breakfast [relative clause]
daam baagenaihka'nna (7) that it is foggy, while it is foggy [relative clause]
daaN (7) someone's, one's [possessive case]
daaN (2) (see **dahaN**)
daan daiboo' dedaigwa'nna (8) written materials (in English); reading
   materials (in English) [nominalized verb]
daan gutsenihka'nna (7) that it is hot, while it is hot [relative clause]

daan newedaigwa'nna (8) speaking (the) Indian (language) [nominal-ized verb]

daa weinna (7) that it is raining, while it is raining [relative clause]

dabai (dabai) (9) sun, day, daytime, clock

dabaidekaH- (8) to eat lunch

dabaidekaneimi'i- (8) to usually go (away) to eat (and then come back, on a daily basis)

dabai'wa (7) all day long [adv]

dabaishu'aiH- (7) to be sunny

    dabaishu'ai-gande (7) to have sunshine

    dabaishu'aihka (7) it is sunny (RESULTATIVE)

dabai'yi (7)/(8) daytime, during the day, noon, at noon [adv]

daga' (-a) (2) friend (male) (archaic) [male speech]

da'ga (4) only, just, but [adv]

dagipoo' (-a) (9) kidney

dahaN (2) our [dual, possessive case, inclusive]

    daha-ba'ande (3) above us two, (high) over us two [dual, inclusive]

dahna- (8) to set (something) down

    nadahna- (8) to be set down (PASSIVE)

    nadahnakandu'i (8) will be set down (FUTURE PASSIVE)

dahwaani (7) spring [noun], in the spring time [adv]

    dahwaa'ni (7) (PAUSAL FORM)

dahwe (2) we [dual, subject case, inclusive]

daiboo' (-a) (2) white person, Euro-American

daiboo'an daigwape (-ha) (3) the English language

daigwa- (3) to speak, talk [intr/tr]

    daigwade (3) speak/speaks (HABITUAL-CUSTOMARY)

    daigwaade (3) (PAUSAL FORM)

daigwape (-ha) (3) language, speech, word(s)

dai'zhi (dai'zhi) (3) sister's husband, brother-in-law [male speech]

daka (9) (alternate form of **dakabi**)

    daka gaba (9) through the snow, in the snow

dakabi (-ta) (7) snow

dakadua'ai- (7) to snow a lot, accumulate (of snow) [intr]

    dakadua'ai'yu (7) it snows a lot, the snow is slowly accumulating (PROGRESSIVE)

dakaweiH- (7) to snow

    dakaweigu (7) while it snowed, when it snowed

    dakáweihwa (7) it snowed (MOMENTANEOUS)

    dakawe'i (7) it snowed (DURATIVE)

damme (2) we [pl, subject case, inclusive]

dammeN (2) our [pl, possessive case, inclusive]
dammen daiboo' ded<u>a</u>igwa'nna (8) (see **daan daiboo' ded<u>a</u>igwa'nna**)
dammen newed<u>a</u>igwa'nna (8) (see **daan newed<u>a</u>igwa'nna**)
dap<u>a</u>ihyaaH- (5) to put on (one's) socks
    dap<u>a</u>ihyahwa (5) put (past) on (one's) socks (MOMENTANEOUS)
dap<u>a</u>ihyaa' (-a) (5) sock(s)
daseweeki' (-a) (9) toe(s)
dawi' (-a) (3) younger brother, younger male cousin
da[']zaN (7) summer [noun], in the summertime [adv]
da'oda- (5) to find [tr]
    da'ota (5) find/finds (DURATIVE)
de<u>a</u>ipede (de<u>a</u>ipedi) (8) child
    dede<u>a</u>ipedee' (-dei') (8) children
de'ase- (7) to be freezing cold (of weather)
    de'aseka (7) it is freezing cold (RESULTATIVE)
deaseN (2) also, too
deboofoi- (8) to study
    deboofoide (8) study/studies, am/is/are a student (HABITUAL-
      CUSTOMARY)
deboo- (8) to write, to draw [tr]
deboogwapi (-ha) (8) writer, journalist, secretary
deche (7)/(9) bad(ly), unpleasant(ly) [adj/adv]
deche gwanaa- (9) to smell bad/unpleasant
deche suaN- (7) to dislike [tr]
    deche suange'nna (7) dislikes/dislike (REPETITIVE)
deche wesunga- (7) to dislike, not feel good about
    deche wesunga' (7) dislikes/dislike, doesn't/don't feel good about
      (DURATIVE)
ded<u>a</u>igwa- (8) to read [intr]
dedakooni' (-a) (8) policeman
dedaposi'igwapi (-ha) (8) carpenter
dede'ai- (8) to work
    dede'a'i (8) work/works (DURATIVE)
dede'ai'i- (8) to work (on a daily basis)
dede'ainukimi'i- (8) to run off to work (on a daily basis)
dede'ainge- (8) to work for (someone/something) (CAUSATIVE)
    dede'ainge'nna (8) work/works for (ITERATIVE)
dedotadawengeN- (9) to cause many holes (in something) [intr]
deesu'a- (6) to feel, be (in a certain mental state)
-degi- (see **-tegi-**)
degumahanningeN- (8) to cook for (someone)

degumahanningebidegua'ai- (8) to usually arrive and go cook for (someone) (on a habitual basis)

degumahannipe (-ha) (4) (oven-baked) bread

degupita' (-a) (3) (electric) light

degwasenge' (-a) (4) frying pan

dehainji (-ha) (2) girl friend [male speech]

deheya' (-a) (4) deer

deheya'an duku (duki) (4) deer meat, venison

dehimbe (-ha) (9) sweetheart

dei' (-a) (2) (female) friend [female speech]

dei'ape' (-a) (3) father's younger brother, uncle

deigu' (-a) (3) a little (bit)

deinde (deindi) (9) (also **deinde'**) little, small [adj]
    deindehwe (deindehi) [dual]
    deindee' (deindei') [pl]

deingu' (-a) (3) (see **deigu'**)

dekaH- (2) to eat [intr/tr]
    dekade (7) eat/eats (CUSTOMARY-HABITUAL)
    dekáfe'nni (4) am/are/is eating (something that does not take very long, such as a snack) (CONTINUATIVE)
    dekákuandu'i (2) will go to eat/going to eat
    deká'yu (4) am/are/is eating (something that takes a while, such as a full meal) (PROGRESSIVE)
    dekáa'yu (PAUSAL FORM)

deka-gahni (-gahni) (8) restaurant

dekape (-ha) (7) eaten [adj], food [noun]

demmaseN/demma (3) then

Dembimbosaage (2) Idaho Falls, Idaho (literally, stone bridge)

dembuiH- (4) to watch [tr]
    dembuihka (4) am/are/is watching (RESULTATIVE)
    dembuitegi- (8) to sit and watch
    dembuiteki sat and watched (DURATIVE)
    dembuitegi'i'yu (8) usually sit(s) and watch(es) (PROGRESSIVE)

-deN (3) (CUSTOMARY-HABITUAL) [verbal suff]

-deN (7) one who [+verb]-s, [verb]-er (dual: **-dehwe**; pl: **-dee'**) [nominal suffix]

denangaH (9) to hear [intr]

denangahka- (9) to hear (STATIVE) [intr]

denangabizhiaN- (4) to obey, learn by listening, behave
    denangabizhiande (4) am/are/is obeying, learning by listening (CUSTOMARY-HABITUAL)

denihani- (8) to judge (someone/something) [tr]

denihanigwapi (-ha) (8) judge, lawyer

denito'ai- (8) to sing [intr]

denito'aigwapi (-ha) (8) singer

dewaseange- (8) to farm [intr]

> **dewaseange'i'yu** (8) farm(s) (on a habitual basis) (PROGRESSIVE)

dewee- (6) to buy

> **deweedu'i** (6) will buy (FUTURE)

deyai- (9) to die

dezahani- (8) to drive (a vehicle), to operate (something) by hand

dezahanigwapi (-ha) (8) driver (of a vehicle)

dezakeena- (8) to sew (something) [tr]

dezakeena'ai- (8) to usually sew

> **dezakeena'ai'yu** (8) am/are/is usually sewing (PROGRESSIVE)

dezateboofoingeH- (8) to teach [intr]

> **dezateboofoinge'nna** (8) teach/teaches [intr] (ITERATIVE)

dezo[']woi (-ha) (4) hat

dogo' (-a) (3) (maternal) grandfather; [male speech]: grandchild(ren) (by one's daughter)

dogwai (8) right (at), exact(ly) [adv]

dogwai-dabai[']yi (8) noon, 12 o'clock P.M.

dogwai-duga[']ni (8) midnight, 12 o'clock 7A.M.

domahanni"- (4) to knead (dough) [intr/tr]

> **domahannipe'nni** (4) am/are/is kneading (dough) (CONTINUATIVE)

do[']mmo (4) winter, in winter, wintertime [adv]

do[']mmo (7) year, winter (here: weather) [noun]

> **egi do[']mmo** (7) this winter

dosa- (6) white [adj pref]

dosabi (9) white [adj] (alternate form of **dosabite**)

> **dosabi naakwai-** (9) to become white

dosabite (dosabiti) (5) white

dowoaH- (7) to be cloudy

> **dowoahka** (7) it is/was cloudy (RESULTATIVE)

doyadaiboo' (-a) (2) Mexican, Mexican-American, Hispanic

do'yoN (-na) (9) neck

> **doo'yoN** (PAUSAL FORM)

do'aiH- (8) to emerge, come out, go out

> **do'aihwa** (8) emerged, came out (MOMENTANEOUS)

dua' (-a) (3) son

dubiichi (-ha) (6) quarter (twenty-five cents)

ducha- (8) dirty [adj pref]

ducha'awo (ducha'awoi') (8) dirty dishes
dudua'nee' (-nei') (9) babies, children
duga'ni (8) night, at night [noun]
dugu (8) must, have to [adv]
duhubite (duhubiti) (5) black
duibichi' (-a) (9) (handsome) young man
dukaN (4)/(5) under [postpos]
dukangu (5) under [postpos]
dukai (5) under [postpos]
duku (duki) (4) meat, flesh, body, mountain sheep
duN (3) in, with, by use of (a language) [postpos]
duu-daiboo' (-a) (2) black person, African-American
duyepe' (-a) (6) boy
du'i (4) will be [postpos]
Dzoon (-ha) (2) John

ede'iN- (7) to be hot
　　ede'inde (7) it is hot (CUSTOMARY-HABITUAL)
ege- (5) new [adj pref]
egebichi (-ha) (7) new
egi (6) now
egi be<u>ai</u>chehku (7) this morning [adv of time]
egi dab<u>ai</u>'yi (7) today [adv of time]
egi dahwani (7) this spring [adv of time]
egi dahwani gimaginde (7) next spring [adv of time]
egi da'za (6) this summer [adv of time]
egi da'zan gimaginde (7) next summer [adv of time]
egi do[']mmo (7) this winter [adv of time]
egi dommo gimaginde (7) next winter [adv of time]
egi yeba'ni (7) this fall [adv of time]
egi yeba'ni gimaginde (7) next fall [adv of time]
egi yeitab<u>ai</u>'yi (7) this afternoon [adv of time]
egi yeika (7) this evening [adv of time]
e[']mmi (4) you [sg, object case]
eN (2) you [sg, object case]
eN (2) your [sg, possessive case]
e[']nne (2) you [sg, subject case]
ezhe'ika'nna (7) that it is cold, while it is cold [relative clause]
ezhe'iN- (7) to be cold [intr]
　　ezhe'inde (ezhe'indi) (7) (it) is cold (CUSTOMARY-HABITUAL)
　　ezhe'inniku (7) as cold (as)

-fe[']nni/-pe[']nni (4) (CONTINUATIVE ASPECT) [verbal suff]

gaba (5) among, between, through
   gaa'ba (PAUSAL FORM)
gaH (5) in, at [postpos]
-gati (5) in (transitive verbs of motion, or movement within a specified
   area; object case of nominalized postpositional phrase) [postpos]
gade- (5) to sit
   gaté (5) am/are/is sitting (DURATIVE)
gadenoo' (gadenoo'a) (3) chair
gagu' (-a) (3) (maternal) grandmother; [female speech]: grandchild(ren)
   (by one's daughter)
gahniN (gahniN) (2) house
gahte (7) at (used with static verbs that indicate no notion)
gahtei' (8) at; people at (a specific location) [pl]
gahtu (2) to [postpos]
   gaahtu (PAUSAL FORM)
gahyunde (8) at
ga'i (9) forehead
ga'imbehe (9) eyebrow(s)
gai (3) not
gai' (2) no
gai himbaigaN (7) not much
gaiháiwa'i (5) it's not there; there's nothing there [expression]
gaisheN (4) not yet
gaisheseN (4) not yet (very informal version of **gaisheN**)
gaiyu'uN (5) late
ga'mmu (-i) (9) jackrabbit
gande (gandi) (4) to have [sing]
   gandehwe (gandehi) to have [dual]
   gandee' (gandei') (9) to have [pl]
gapai (gapai) (5) bed
gapii' (-a) (7) coffee
gasa (gasai) (9) wing
gebedande (gebedandi) (7) long
gedii' (-a) (4) cat
-ge'nna (4) (REPETITIVE ASPECT) [verbal suff]
genduN (7) yesterday [adj]
gendum beaichehku (7) yesterday morning [adv of time]
gendu yeika (7) yesterday evening [adv of time]
gendu yeitabai'yi (7) yesterday afternoon [adv of time]

genga (gengai) (6) onion
genu' (-a) (3) (paternal) grandfather; [male speech]: grandchild(ren)
   (by one's son)
gesunga- (7) to like (by tasting with the mouth); to taste
   deche gesunga- (7) to not like (by tasting with the mouth)
getaaN (7) very, really, extremely [adv]
getande (getandi) (9) hard [adj] [sing]
gewagaH (5) next to, beside [postpos]
gewagahku (5) next to (transitive verbs of motion, or movement
   toward) [postpos]
gia' (5) maybe, perhaps
giase['lba (5) maybe, perhaps
gizhaa (4) not good (=**gai tsaa'**)
godokoN (-na) (9) necklace
go'hai (go'hai) (9) intestines
goobai (goobai) (9) face
   goo'bai (PAUSAL FORM)
gooni- (7) to go and come back, to make a round trip [intr]
gooni- (8) to make a circle, cycle [intr]
goonipe (8) cycled; gone (around) in a circle (PERFECT ASPECT)
gotoo- (4) to make fire [intr]
gotoope (-ha) (4) fire
gotoonoo' (-a) (4) stove
gozho['lhai- (8) to wash (something) [tr]
go'aiH- (8) to return, go back, come back
go'aihki- (8) to come home (from perspective of speaker)
go'aihkimi'i- (8) to usually come home (on a habitual basis)
-gu (7) while, when [subordinator]
guchuN (guchuna) (4) cow
guhnaiki- (4) to run (toward the speaker)
   guhnáikingu (4) is running (toward the speaker) (MOMENTANEOUS)
      [intr]
gu['lna (gu['lna) (4) wood
gunawaimungu (gunawaimungi) (8) train, boxcar, railroad
gupa (4) in, within [postpos]
gupángu (5) in, within (transitive verbs of motion, or movement
   toward) [postpos]
gusa (gusai) (5) pants
gutseniH- (7) to heat up, get hot
   gutsénihka (7) it heats up, it gets hot, it heated up, it got hot
      (RESULTATIVE)

gutsenihka'ai- (7) to be continuously hot (of the weather) [intr]
    gutsenihka'ai'yu (7) it is continuously hot (PROGRESSIVE)
guyungwi'yaa' (-a) (4) turkey
guyungwi'yaa'an duku (duki) (4) turkey (meat)
-gwa- (8) (indicates direction away from the speaker) (AUXILIARY VERB)
gwahaintsuhni (gwahaintsuhni) (9) spine, backbone
gwanaa"- (9) to smell [intr]
    gwanaade (9) it smells (CUSTOMARY-HABITUAL)
gwasu'uN (-na) (4) dress, skirt, shirt, blouse
gwee' (gwehi) (6) wife
gwehe (gwehi) (6) wife [alternative form]
gwida-gahni (gwida-gahni) (2) bathroom, restroom [male speech]
gwidape (-ha) (9) feces, shit
gwiipusiaH- (7) to be smoky (of the environment)
    gwiipusiahka (7) it is smoky, it was smoky (RESULTATIVE)

ha (3) [question particle]
haa' (2) yes
ha['lbi- (3)/(8) to lie, be (in a supine position), lie down, go to bed
    habikwai'nna (8) usually go/goes to bed (ITERATIVE)
    hap' (5) am/is/are lying (in a supine position) (DURATIVE)
haga' (5) where?
haga'ahti? (8) where at?
hagadeN (2) who?
    hagaadeN (PAUSAL FORM)
hagadeN (5) which . . . ? [+ noun]
hagai' (3) how? what?
    hagai' enne? (6) what do you mean?
hagaiti (5) how? what? (transitive verbs of motion, or movement within
    a specified area; object of nominalized postpositional phrase)
haganai' (2) (from) where?
haganaite (2) (from) where? (a specific placename)
haganni (5) how? in what way? what? (nonmaterial)
    haganni naakwa? (6) what happened?
hagannihatu (5) how? in what way? what? (nonmaterial) (intransitive
    verb of motion, movement toward or into specified area)
haganni'yunde (4) why? how come?
hagapundu (2) (to) where?
haga'ahku (5) where?
haga'al'lnna (4) where?
    haga'aa'nna (PAUSAL FORM)

hainji (-ha) (2) (male) friend

ha'nii' (-a) (9) beaver

ha[']nniibe (-ha) (4) (Indian) corn, maize

hanni- (3) to do [intr/tr]

    hanni'yu (4) am/are/is doing (progressive)

hannii'yu (PAUSAL FORM)

hannihkaN- (9) to be situated/located (STATIVE)

    hannihkande (9) is situated/located (STATIVE, CUSTOMARY-HABITUAL)

hap' (5) am/is/are lying (in a supine position) (DURATIVE) (see **ha[']bi-**)

ha[']lyangenaa' (8) first, first (thing)

hibi- (7) to drink

    hibi'nna (7) that . . . is/are drinking [subordinating suff]

himb_ai_' (8) when?

himb_ai_gaN (6) how much?

    g_ai_ himb_ai_gaN (7) not much

himb_ai_gande (6) how much?

himb_ai_gandee' (himb_ai_gandei') (6) how many?

himb_ai_gandengahtu (6) for how much (money)?

    himb_ai_'gaandengahtu (PAUSAL FORM)

hinga dab_ai_ (8) what time (of day)?

    hinga dab_ai_ naha'yu? (8) what time (of day) is it?

hi[']nni (hi[']nna) (4) what?

hiwange- (6) to pick up (things) with the hands; select (from a pile)

    hiwangekuandu'i (6) will go and pick (things) up with the hands
        (FUTURE)

hoda- (9) to dig

    hoo'da- (PAUSAL FORM)

    hodade usually dig/digs (CUSTOMARY-HABITUAL)

hoih (9) around, encircling [postpos]

hubia' (-a) (9) song, music

hukun_eai_H- (7) to blow dust [intr]

    hukun_ea_ife'nni (7) it is blowing dust (CONTINUATIVE)

hutsi' (-a) (3) (paternal) grandmother; [female speech]: grandchild(ren)
    (by one's son)

huu-baga (-na) (9) arrow

huukuN (-na) (9) collarbone

-'i- (8) (indicates periodic repetitive or habitual action) [prefinal verbal
    suff]

idee' (7) these (close enough to touch) [pl, subject case]

ideeN (7) their (close enough to touch) [pl, possessive case]

idei' (7) these (close enough to touch) [pl, object case]

ideheN (7) these (two) (close enough to touch) [dual, possessive case]

idehi (7) these (two) (close enough to touch) [dual, object case]

idehwe (7) these (two) (close enough to touch) [dual, subject case]

ideN (3)/(7) this (close enough to touch) [sing, subject case]

ika (7) this (close enough to touch) [sing, object case]

ikaN (7) this (close enough to touch) [sing, possessive case]

iki (4) right here [adv of place]

iki ma'i (4) here it is

isheN (2)/(3) this (close enough to touch) (contrastive) [sing, subject case]

iwaa' (7) tomorrow [adv of time]

iwaa' be<u>ai</u>chehku (7) tomorrow morning [adv of time] (see also **be<u>ai</u>chehku**)

iwaa' duga'ni (7) tomorrow night [adv of time] (see also **duga'ni**)

iwaa' yeika (7) tomorrow evening [adv of time] (see also **yeika**)

iwaa' yeitab<u>ai</u>'yi (7) tomorrow afternoon [adv of time] (see also **yeitab<u>ai</u>'yi**)

izhape' (-a) coyote

-ka (3) (RESULTATIVE ASPECT) [verbal suff]

-kandeN (9) (STATIVE) [verbal suff]

-ki (4) [+ verb]-ed and just arrived (AUXILIARY VERB)

-ku (5) (MOMENTANEOUS ASPECT) [verbal suff] (variant of **-kwa/-hwa**)

-kua' (5) go and [+verb] (AUXILIARY VERB)

-kwa (5) (MOMENTANEOUS APSECT) [verbal suff] (variant of **-kwa** and **-ku**)

-kwai'nna (8) habitually [+verb] (variant of **-hwai'nna**)

ma (4)/(5) this/that, it (visible)

-ma'<u>ai</u>H (2) with, in addition to

ma'<u>ai</u>hku (6) with, in addition to (variant of **ma'<u>ai</u>H**)

maa[']nangwaH (5) behind (behind something and away from speaker) [postpos]

maa[']nangwahku (5) behind (transitive verbs of motion, movement toward speaker) [postpos]

mabizhiaN- (4) to fix with the hands [tr]

made (7) this/that (neutral distance) [sing, subject case]

madee' (7) these, those (neutral distance) [pl, subject case]

madeeN (7) their (neutral distance) [pl, possessive case]

madeheN (7) this/that (neutral distance) [dual, possessive case]

madehi (7) this/that (neutral distance) [dual, object case]

madehwe (7) this/that (neutral distance) [dual, subject case]

madei' (7) this/that (neutral distance) [pl, object case]

madeN (3)/(7) this/that (neutral distance) [sing, possessive case]

magozho'hai- (8) to wash with the hand(s)

-mahwaka (8) after finish [+ verb]-ing (AUXILIARY VERB)

mai (3) they say, people say, it is said [quotative particle]

-ma'i (6) (variant of **ma'aiH**)

maiku (2) okay, alright

maitenga (5) outside [adv of place]

maitengaku (5) outside (transitive verbs of motion, movement toward speaker) [adv of place]

maitengate (7) outside (used with static verbs that indicate no motion) [adv of place]

maka (7) this/that (neutral distance) [sing, object case]

makaN (7) this/that (neutral distance) [sing, possessive case]

maN (5) on, with (instrument)

manegiseemote (manegiseemoti) (6) fifty [numeral]

manegitee' (manegitei') (6) five (of something) [noun]

maseange- (8) to plant, sow, raise (animals) [tr]

maseN (3) this/that (neutral distance) (contrastive) [sing, subject case]

mase'a (8) plant/plants, sow/sows, raise/raises (animals) (DURATIVE) [tr]

meheN (2) your [dual]

mehwe (2) you [dual]

memme (2) you [pl]

memmeN (2) your [pl]

mia' (3) let's go (see **mi'a-**)

mi'a- (2) to go [intr]

    mi'a'yu (2) am/are/is walking [sing & pl]

    mi'aa'yu (PAUSAL FORM)

    mimi'a'yu [miwi'a'yu] (2) (dual form of **mi'a'yu**)

mi'awa'iH- (5) to go out

    mi'awa'ihyu (5) going out (PROGRESSIVE)

-mi'i- (8) (indicates habitual, repeated action) [verbal suff]

mimi'a'yu [miwi'a'yu] (3) (dual form of **mi'a'yu**)

mu'bii (-ha) (4) car, automobile

mubishipe (-ha) (9) snot, nasal mucus

mumbichi (-ha) (9) owl

munna'gwa (7) last year [adv of time]

    munnaa'gwa (PAUSAL FORM)

munnagwa dahwani (7) last spring [adv of time]

munnagwa da'za (7) last summer [adv of time]

munnagwa dommo (7) last winter [adv of time]
munnagwa yeba'ni (7) last fall [adv of time]
muu'bi (1)/(9) nose
muubindadawennaN (-na) (9) nostrils

na- (8) (PASSIVE) [verbal pref]
-'nna (4) (ITERATIVE ASPECT) [verbal suff]
naa- (6) to happen, become, be, do (variant of **naha-**)
naafaite (naafaiti) (6) six
naafaitee' (naafaitei') (6) six (of something)
naafaitenga daa naakihka (8) at six (o'clock)
naakaN- (9) to live, exist [intr]
naakiH- (8) to become, get to be (in time)
    naakihka (8) (it) becomes (in time), gets to be (in time) (RESULTATIVE)
naakwai- (9) to become
    dosabi naakwai- (9) to become white
nabuiH- (5) to be seen, be, look (like) (passive of **bui-**)
    nabuinde (5) look/looks (like), is/are (seen) (HABITUAL-CUSTOMARY)
    -ni nabuinde (9) (it) looks like/ (it) looks [+ adj]
nadainape' (-a) (3) husband; sister's husband [female speech]
nadahna- (8) to be set down (passive of **dahna-**)
    nadahnakandu'i (8) will be set down (FUTURE)
nadatewade (nadatewadi) (6) package, carton
    nadatewaate (PAUSAL FORM)
nade'asengepe (-ha) (6) frozen [adj], something frozen [noun]
nade'eyan nasu'waiN- (9) to be shy [intr]
    nade'eyan nasu'wainde (9) am/is/are shy (CUSTOMARY-HABITUAL)
nadewaga- (6)/(8) to sell
    nadewagahwa (6) sold (MOMENTANEOUS)
nadewagagwapi (-ha) (8) cashier, vendor, merchant
nadewengahni (nadewengahni) (8) store
nado'aigahni (nado'aigahni) (5) bathroom, restroom, toilet [female speech]
nagozho['lhai- (8) to bathe [intr]
    nagozhohaineitsi (8) after have gone and bathed (on a daily basis)
naha- (5) to do, make, happen [intr] (alternate form of **naa-**)
nahape (7) has become (PERFECTIVE)
nai' (2) from [postpos]
naingiH (-ha) (9) ear
naite (2) from [+ place-name] [postpos]
nambe (nambeha/nampeha) (4) shoe

nammi' (-a) (3) younger sister

nanambuipe (-ha) (9) footprint(s)

nanangaH- (9) to be heard, sound (PASSIVE)

    nanangahkandeN (9) is heard (PASSIVE, STATIVE)

nangaH- (9) to hear

nangasumbaaduH- (3) to understand (by hearing) [tr]

    nangasumbaaduhka (3) understand/understands (RESULTATIVE)

naniha (nanihai) (2) name

naniha- (3) to be named/called

    nanihade (3) is called, be named (CUSTOMARY-HABITUAL)

    nanihaade (PAUSAL FORM)

naninakai- (6) to cost

    naninakaide (6) it costs (CUSTOMARY-HABITUAL)

nanimee- (6) to cost

    nanimede (6) it costs (CUSTOMARY-HABITUAL)

    nanimeete (PAUSAL FORM)

nasundeganaaH- (7) to plan (something)

    nasundeganaahka (7) plan/plans (RESULTATIVE)

natesu'uN (-na) (8) medicine

natesu'ungahni (natesu'ungahni) (8) hospital

nawasoaH- (8) to get dressed [intr]

    nawasoa' (8) put on your clothes! (IMPERATIVE)

    nawasoahwai'nna (8) habitually get/gets dressed

    nawasoakua' (8) go and put on your clothes!

nawa'aipe' (-a) (3) wife; brother's wife [male speech]

nazatewa' (-a) (3) door

nazawaiyiH- (5) to hang [intr]

    nazawaiyihka (5) am/is/are hanging (RESULTATIVE)

ne (2) I, my

neai (9) me [object case]

neai"- (7) to blow (of wind), be windy

    ne'ai (7) it is/was windy (DURATIVE)

    neaide (neaidi) (7) it is windy (CUSTOMARY-HABITUAL)

    neaipe'nni (7) it is windy (CONTINUATIVE)

neaN (2) my, mine [emphatic] [sing, possessive case]

neheN (2) our [dual, possessive case, exclusive]

nehwe (2) we [dual, subject case, exclusive]

-nei- (8) to go and [+VERB] and return (AUXILIARY VERB)

-nei' (5) left (to do something) and came back [verbal suff]

nemme (2) we [pl, subject case, exclusive]

nemmeN (2) our [pl, possessive case, exclusive]

nemmi (8) us, for us [pl, object case, exclusive]

ne[']we (ne[']wi) (3) person, Indian, Shoshoni (Indian)

newedaigwape (-ha) (8) the Indian people's language

ne[']we duN (3) in (the) Shoshoni/Indian (language), through the Indian/Shoshoni language

neweguchu (-na) (2) buffalo

newezoiga'i (-ha) (2) Nez Perce (Indian)

niikwi- (5) to tell, say [intr/tr]

    niikwi (5) said, told (MOMENTANEOUS)

    niigwi'nna (5) telling, saying (to) (ITERATIVE)

-niku (7) like . . . , as . . . [postpos]

noha (6) used to

noondea (8) or else, otherwise

no'yo (no'yi) (6) egg

noo'yo (noo'yi) (6) testicle

nukiN- (8) to run

nukigi- (9) to run (toward the speaker)

nukigwai'i- (9) to run fast (with randome movement) [intr]

nuk'ndemma (5) just go then! [expression]

odee' (7) that [pl, subject case]

odeeN (7) that [pl, possessive case]

odei' (7) that [pl, object case]

odeheN (7) that [dual, possessive case]

odehi (7) that [dual, object case]

odehwe (7) that [dual, subject case]

odeN (3)/(7) that [sing, subject case]

ogwaideN (7) flowing [adj], river, stream [noun]

ohapite (ohapiti) (5) yellow

    o'ohapitee' (5) yellow [pl]

oka (7) that [sing, object case]

okaN (7) that [sing, possessive case]

oku (7) there [adv of place]

ondembite (ondembiti) (5) brown

oseN (3) that (contrastive) [sing, subject case]

oyoseN (6) always

-pe (7) (PERFECTIVE ASPECT) [verbal suff]

-pe[']nni/-fe[']nni (4) (CONTINUATIVE ASPECT) [verbal suff]

saape (-ha) (4) stew

sa[']bai (5) in there

sadee' (7) that (within sight) (specific) [pl, subject case]

sadee' (sadee'a) (4) dog

sadeeN (7) that (within sight) (specific) [pl, possessive case]

sadeheN (7) that (within sight) (specific) [dual, possessive case]

sadehi (7) that (within sight) (specific) [dual, object case]

sadehwe (7) that (within sight) (specific) [dual, subject case]

sadei' (7) that (within sight) (specific) [pl, object case]

sadeN (7) that (within sight) (specific) [sing, subject case]

saidee' (7) this (not close enough to touch) (specific) [pl, subject case]

saideeN (7) this (not close enough to touch) (specific) [pl, possessive case]

saideheN (7) this (not close enough to touch) (specific) [dual, possessive case]

saidehi (7) this here (not close enough to touch) (specific) [dual, object case]

saidehwe (7) this here (not close enough to touch) (specific) [dual, subject case]

saidei' (7) this (not close enough to touch) (specific) [pl, object case]

saideN (7)   his here (not close enough to touch) (specific) [sing, subject case]

Saigwi'ogwai' (2) Bannock Creek (Fort Hall Reservation) (also **Saigwihunu'**)

saika (7) this here, (not close enough to touch) (specific) [sing, object case]

saikaN (7) this here (not close enough to touch) (specific) [sing, possessive case]

saiki (7) here (not close enough to touch) (specific) [adv of place]

saitu (8) over here [adv of place]

saka (7) that (within sight) (specific) [sing, object case]

sakaN (7) that (within sight) (specific) [sing, possessive case]

saku (7) over there (specific) [adv of place]

sape (-ha) (9) stomach

sea"- (9) to grow [tr/intr]

seahkaN- (9) to grow (STATIVE) [intr]

se[']ba (5) maybe, perhaps

sebagia' (5) maybe, perhaps

seemote (seemoti) (6) ten [numeral]

sehedukubichi (-ha) (9) bobcat

semme' (-a) (6) one [numeral]

sengwaibiN (6) (see **u sengwaibiN**)

sesewe' (8) sometimes

sewe (6) one (alternate of **seme'**)

sii-bungu (sii-bungi) (4) sheep

sii-bungudaiboo' (-a) (2) Basque

sidee' (7) this (close enough to touch) (specific) [pl, subject case]

sideeN (7) this (close enough to touch) (specific) [pl, possessive case]

sidei' (7) this (close enough to touch) (specific) [pl, object case]

sideheN (7) this (close enough to touch) (specific) [dual, possessive case]

sidehi (7) this (close enough to touch) (specific) [dual, object case]

sidehwe (7) this (close enough to touch) (specific) [dual, subject case]

sideN (7) this (close enough to touch) (specific) [sing, subject case]

sika (7) this (close enough to touch) (specific) [sing, object case]

sikaN (7) this (close enough to touch) (specific) [sing, possessive case]

siki (7) right here (specific) [adv of place]

sikiteN (7) right here [adv of place]

sodee' (7) that (specific) [pl, subject case]

sodeeN (7) that (specific) [pl, possessive case]

sodeheN (7) that (specific) [dual, possessive case]

sodehi (7) that (specific) [dual, object case]

sodehwe (7) that (specific) [dual, subject case]

sodei' (7) that (specific) [pl, object case]

sodeN (7) that (specific) [sing, subject case]

sogo (9) (alternate form of **sogope**)

    sogo ba'a (9) on land, on the ground

sogope (-ha) (9) land, ground, earth

soho[']bi (-ta) (4) tree

soka (7) that (specific) [sing, object case]

sokaN (7) that (specific) [sing, possessive case]

soku (7) there (specific) [adv of place]

so'o (so'i) (9) cheek(s)

sooN (7) a lot, much, many [adv quantifier]

soonde (soondi) much, many [sing]

    soondehwe (soondehi) much, many [dual]

    soondee' (soondei') much, many [pl]

Soo-gahni (2) Blackfoot (Idaho) (literally, many houses)

sooseN (7) a lot, much

sosoni' (-a) (2) Shoshoni (Indian)

soto (7) over that way [adv of place]

sowoN (-na) (9) lung(s)

    soo'woH (PAUSAL FORM)

suaN- (7) to think, want, feel, need [tr]
    su'a (6) thinking, think/thinks (DURATIVE)
-suaN- (9) to want to [+ verb] (AUXILIARY VERB)
subai' (8) then
su['] bai' (8) in there
sudee' (7) that (out of sight) (specific) [pl, subject case]
sudeeN (7) that (out of sight) (specific) [pl, possessive case]
sudeheN (7) that (out of sight) (specific) [dual, possessive case]
sudehi (7) that (out of sight) (specific) [dual, object case]
sudehwe (7) that (out of sight) (specific) [dual, subject case]
sudei' (7) that (out of sight) (specific) [pl, object case]
sudeN (7) that (out of sight) (specific) [sing, subject case]
suka (7) that (out of sight) (specific) [sing, object case]
sukaN (7) that (out of sight) (specific) [sing, possessive case]
suku (7) there (out of sight) (specific) [adv of place]
(gai) sumbana'i- (4) to not know [intr/tr]
    gai sumbana'i'nna (4) know not/knows not (ITERATIVE)
sunni'yunde (6) that's why [conjunction] (variant form: **sunnihyunde**)
suwai- (6) to want, need
    suwa'i (6) want/wants, need/needs (DURATIVE) (implies that there
      are only one or two items to choose from)
    suwa'ihka (6) want/wants, need/needs (RESULTATIVE) (implies
      large selection of items to choose from)
su'ahaibei- (7) to mess up [tr]
    su'ahaibeideN (7) someone who messes things up (HABITUAL-
      CUSTOMARY)
    su'ahaibeidee' (7) people who mess things up [pl]
    su'ahaidehwe (7) people who mess things up [dual]
su'ana (8) at, about, around, usually [adv of time] (used with expres-
  sions of time)
    su'aa'na (PAUSAL FORM)

-teese (6) only . . . (added to numbers)
-tegi-/-degi- (8) to start (to), begin (to); be (in a place), be seated; put
  (AUXILIARY VERB)
tsa- (5) by hand, with the hands [instrumental pref]
tsaa-baingwi (tsaa-baingwi) (4) mountain trout
tsaa-dekape (-ha) (9) favorite food
tsaaN (4) good, well
tsaan deesu'a (6) (it) feels good, (it) has a good outlook (DURATIVE)
tsaandetsi' (-a) (6) nice, little kid

tsaangesunga- (7) to like the taste of (something)

tsaangu beaichehku (2) good morning (variant form: **tsaangu baiche**)

tsaangu yeitabai'yi/yeitatabai'yi (2) good afternoon

tsaangu yeyeika (2) good evening

tsaasuaN- (7) to like, think well of [tr]
> **tsaasuange'nna** (7) likes/like (REPETITIVE)

tsaawesunga- (7) to feel good about (something), like (something)
> **tsaawesunga'** (7) feels/feel good about, likes/like (DURATIVE)

tsadamani (-ha) (3) Chinese (person), Chinese (language)

tsateboofoiN- (8) to teach
> **tsateboofo'i** (8) teach/teaches, am/is/are teaching (DURATIVE)

tsateboofoingeH- (8) to teach (something) [tr]
> **tsateboofoingehwai'nna** (8) teach/teaches on a daily basis
> **tsateboofoinge'nna** (8) teach/teaches, am/is/are teaching (something) [intr]

tsateboofoingedegimi'i- (8) to start teaching (something) on a daily
basis

tsategi- (5) to put by hand [tr]
> **tsategi-nei'** (5) went and put it (and has/have returned)

tsa'utu"- (5) to give (something) by hand [tr]

tsayaahki- (4) to carry with both hands down low [tr]
> **tsayaahki** (4) carry (it) with both hands down low (IMPERATIVE)

-tsi (8) after having [+ verb] [verbal suff]

tsiambe (-ha) (6) tomato

tsinna' (-a) (4) potatoes
> **tsiinna'** (PAUSAL FORM)

tsitsugaH- (9) to point at, point out [tr]

tsoape (-ha) (9) shoulder(s)

tso'ape (-ha) (5) ghost

tsugupe' (-a) (6) old man

u (3)/(4) him, her, it, them (someone/thing already mentioned) [object
case]
> **u sengwaibi** (6) half (used only in reference to money)
> **u sengwaibi ma'ai** (6) fifty cents (literally, with half of it [a dollar]

udee' (7) that (out of sight) [pl, subject case]

udeeN (7) that (out of sight) [pl, possessive case]

udehi (7) that (out of sight) [dual, object case]

udehwe (7) that (out of sight) [dual, subject case]

udei' (7) that (out of sight) [pl, object case]

udeN (3) that (out of sight) [sing, subject case]

uka (5) that (out of sight) [sing, object case]
ukaN (5) that (out of sight) [sing, possessive case]
uku (7) there (out of sight) [adv of place]
ukuhti (6) there [adv]
useN (3) that (out of sight) (CONTRASTIVE) [sing, subject case]
utu" (5) to give

waapi (-ta) (4) (Utah) juniper tree (also called cedar tree in southern Idaho)
wagande (wagandi) (9) at (someone's), at (something's) [noun]
waahni' (-a) (6) fox
wa'aiH (9) like [conj, postpos] (alternate form of **wa'iH**)
wahambiaseemote (wahambiaseemoti) (6) two hundred [numeral]
wahatehwe (wahatehi) (6) two [numeral]
wahyaN- (7) to burn
wahyande (wahyandi) (7) fire
wa'iH (9) like (something) [conj, postpos]
    wa'i nabuinde (9) (it) looks like (something)
wanadeboope (-ha) (6) dollar
watsewite (watsewiti) (6) four [numeral]
watsewiteese (6) only four
wazi- (9) to hide (something) [tr]; hide, be hidden [intr]
wazika- (9) to hide oneself, be hidden [intr]
wei- (7) to rain
    we'i (7) it rained (DURATIVE)
wei'i- (7) to rain (periodically over time)
    wei'ide (7) it rains (periodically over time) (HABITUAL-CUSTOMARY)
    wei'iite (PAUSAL FORM)
wenangwa (5) in front of [postpos]
wenangwaku (5) in front of [postpos]
we[']ne- (5) to stand
    we[']nne (5) am/is/are standing (DURATIVE)
wepagu'i- (4) to chop, split
    wepagu'i'nna (4) am/are/is chopping (ITERATIVE)
    wepagu'ii'nna (PAUSAL FORM)
wepa'i- (8) to hit
wesunga- (7) to feel (something) with body
wihyu (2) then, and then, but
witua' (wituai') (8) drum, pot
witua-wepa'igwapi (-ha) (8) drummer
witu-wepa'aiN- (9) to drum [intr]

wizha (7) should, might [adv]
wobindotadegi' (-a) (9) northern flicker
wongo[']bi (-ta) (4) pine tree
    wongoo'bi (PAUSAL FORM)

ya'iH- (9) to enter, go in [intr]
    ya'ihwa- (9) to go down (of sun), set (of sun) [intr]
yamba (yamba̱i) (4) wild carrots (yampa root)
yamba'i (-ha) (2) Kiowa (Indian), Southern Plains Indian
yebaani (7) fall, autumn [noun], in the fall/autumn [adv]
    yebaa'ni (PAUSAL FORM)
yeitaba̱i[']yi (8) afternoon; in the afternoon [adv]
yeze- (8) to get up, fly [intr]
    yetse (8) is getting up, got up (DURATIVE)
    yezegwaH-/yezekuaH- (9) to fly away (from the speaker)
    yezemi'i'yu (8) get/gets up (on a daily basis) (PROGRESSIVE)
-[']yu (3)/(4) (PROGRESSIVE ASPECT) [verbal suff]
yuhudegumahannipe (-ha) (4) fry bread
yuhupe (-ha) (7) fat
yu'nainde (yu'naindi) (9) soft [adj]
    yu'naindehwe (yu'naindehi) soft [dual]
    yu'naindee' (yu'naindei') soft [pl]
yuuta' (-a) (2) Ute (Indian)

Daiboo' – Sosoni' d<u>ai</u>gwape ma'<u>ai</u>
English – Shoshoni Glossary

about (of time) **su'ana**
above **ba'ande**
above us two **daha-ba'ande**
accumulate (of snow), to **dakadua'<u>ai</u>-**
African-American **duu-daiboo' (-a)**
after finish [+ verb]-ing **-mahwaka**
afternoon **yeitab<u>ai</u>'yi/yeitatab<u>ai</u>'yi**
afternoon, this **egi yeitab<u>ai</u>'yi**
afternoon, tomorrow **iwaa' yeitab<u>ai</u>'yi**
afternoon, yesterday **gendu yeitab<u>ai</u>'yi**
a little (bit) **deigu' (-a)/deingu' (-a)**
all day long **dab<u>ai</u>'wa**
alright **m<u>ai</u>ku**
a long time ago **be<u>ai</u>m bee; be<u>ai</u>N**
a lot **sooN; sooseN**
already **b<u>ai</u>sheN**
also **deaseN**
always **oyoseN**
among **gaba**
ant(s) **aani**
apple **aapo' (-a)**
around [postpos] **hoih**
around (of time) **su'ana**
arrive, to **bide-**
arrive and [+ verb], to **-bide-**
arrived, has/have **bidennu**
arrow **huu-baga (-na)**
as . . . **-niku**
at **-b<u>ai</u>du/-b<u>ai</u>tu; gaH; gahte; gahyunde; su'ana; wagande (wagandi)**
at night **duga'ni**
at noon **dab<u>ai</u>'yi**

aunt (paternal) **baha' (-a)**
automobile **mu'bii (-ha)**
autumn **yebaa'ni**

babies **dudua'nee' (-nei')**
back [adv] **bituseN**
backbone **gwahaintsuhni**
bad(ly) **deche**
Bannock (Indian) **bannaite' (-a)**
Bannock Creek (Fort Hall Reservation) **Saigwi'ogwai'**
Basque **sii-bungudaiboo' (-a)**
bathe, to **nagozho'hai-**
bathroom **nado'aigahni (nado'aigahni); gwida-gahni (gwida-gahni)**
be, to **naa-**
be (in a certain mental state), to **deesu'a-**
be (in a place), to **-tegi-**
be (in a supine position), to **ha'bi-**
be (like), to **nabuiH-**
be (of time), to get to **naakiH-**
be named/called, to **naniha-**
be seated, to **-tegi-**
be windy, to **neai-**
beaver **ha'nii' (-a)**
become, to **naa-; naakiH-; naha-; naakwai-**
bed **gapai (gapai)**
begin (to), to **-tegi-**
behave, to **denangabizhiaN-**
behind (facing speaker) **binnangwa**
behind (facing away from speaker) **maa'nangwaH**
beside **baihyugi; gewaga**
between **gaba**
big **biaichi' (-a), bibiaichinehwe (-nehi), bibiaichi' (-a); bia-**
bison **bozhe'na (bozhe'nai); neweguchu (-na); biaguchu (-na)**
bit, a **deigu' (-a)/deingu' (-a)**
black **duhubite (duhubiti)**
Blackfoot (Indian) **baki'ehe' (-a)**
Blackfoot (Idaho) **Soo-gahni**
black person **duu-daiboo' (-a)**
blood **beepi (-ta)**
blouse **gwasu'uN (gwasu'una)**
blow (dust), to **hukuneaiH-**

blow (wind), to **ne<u>ai</u>-**
blue **<u>ai</u>behibite (<u>ai</u>behibiti)**
bobcat **sehedukubichi (-ha)**
boxcar **gunawaimungu (gunawaimungi)**
boy **duyepe' (-a)**
bread (oven baked) **degumahanipe (-ha)**
breakfast **daadekape (-ha)**
breakfast, to eat **daadekaH-**
breast **bizhi' (-a)**
brother (father's older) **bia'ape' (-a)**
brother (father's younger) **dei'ape' (-a)**
brother (mother's) **ada' (-a)**
brother (older) **babi' (-a)**
brother (younger) **dawi' (-a)**
brother-in-law [male speech] **d<u>ai</u>'zhi (d<u>ai</u>'zhi)**
brother's wife **bahambia' (-a); nawa'<u>ai</u>pe'**
brown **ondembite (ondembiti)**
buffalo **bozhe'na (bozhe'n<u>ai</u>); neweguchu (-na); biaguchu (-na)**
burn, to **wahyaN-**
but **da'ga; wihyu**
butter **bizhi'yuhu (bizhi'yuhi)**
buy, to **dewee-**
by use of (a language) **duN**

called, to be **naniha-**
camas root **basigoo' (-a)**
carpenter **dedaposi'igwapi (-ha)**
carton **nadatewade (nadatewadi)**
cashier **nadewagagwapi (-ha)**
cat **gedii' (-a)**
car **mu'bii (-ha)**
carrots (wild) **yamba (yamb<u>ai</u>)**
carry (with both hands down low), to **tsayaahki-**
cedar tree (Utah juniper) **waapi (-ta)**
chair **gadenoo' (-a)**
cheek **so'o (so'i)**
child **de<u>ai</u>pede (de<u>ai</u>pedi)**
children **ded<u>eai</u>pedee' (-dei'); dudua'nee' (-nei')**
Chinese (person or language) **tsadamani (-ha)**
chop, to **wepagu'i-**
circle, to make a **gooni-**

clock **dabai**
cloudy, to be **dowoaH-**
coat **biagwasu'u (-na)**
coffee **gapii' (-a)**
cold, to be **ezhe'iN-**
cold, to be freezing **de'ase-**
collar bone **huukuN (-na)**
come back, to **go'aiH-**
come home, to **go'aihki-**
come home, to usually **go'aihkimi'i-**
come out, to **do'aiH-**
cook for, to **degumahaningeN-**
corn (Indian), maize **ha[']nniibe (-ha)**
cost, to **naninakai-; nanimee-**
cousin (older female) **bazi' (-a)**
cousin (male) **ada' (-a)**
cousin (younger male) **dawi' (-a)**
cow **guchuN (guchuna)**
cow (female); milk cow **bizhi'guchuN (bizhi'guchuna)**
coyote **izhape' (-a)**
Crow Indian **a'aa' (-a)**
cycle, to **gooni-**
cycled **goonipe**

daughter **baide' (-a); baide (baidi)**
daughter (brother's) [female speech] **baha' (-a)**
daughter (sister's) [male speech] **ada' (-a)**
day **dabai**
day, during the **dabai'yi**
daytime **dabai'yi; dabai**
deer **deheya' (-a)**
deer meat **deheya'an duku (duki)**
die, to **deyai-**
die of hunger, to **bahodeyai-**
differently **andapuN**
dig, to **hoda-**
dirty **ducha-**
dirty dishes **ducha'awo (ducha'awoi')**
dish **a[']lwo (awoi')**
dishes, dirty **ducha'awo (ducha'awoi')**
dislike, to **deche suaN-; deche wesunga-**

do, to **naa-; naha-; hanni-**
dog **sadee' (-a)**
dollar **wanadeboope (-ha)**
door **nazatewa' (-a)**
draw, to **deboo-**
dress **gwasu'uN (gwasu'una)**
dressed, to get **nawasoaH-**
drink, to **hibi-**
drive (a vehicle), to **dezahani-**
driver **dezahanigwapi (-ha)**
drum **witua' (wituai')**
drum, to [intr] **witu-wepa'aiN-**
drummer **witua-wepa'igwapi (-ha)**
dry, to be/become **basakwai-**
dry up, to **basa-**
dust, to blow **hukuneaiH-**

ear **naingiH (-ha)**
early morning **beaichehku**
early in the morning **beaichehkuseN**
earth **sogo, sogope**
eat, to **dekaH-**
eaten **dekape (-ha)**
eat breakfast, to **daadekaH-**
eat lunch, to **dabaidekaH-**
egg **no'yo (no'yi)**
electric light **degupita' (-a)**
else, or **noondea**
emerge, to **do'aiH-**
English (language) **daiboo'an daigwape (-ha)**
enter, to **ya'iH-**
Euramerican **daiboo' (-a)**
evening, this **egi yeika**
evening, tomorrow **iwaa' yeika**
evening, yesterday **gendu yeika**
exact(ly) **dogwai**
exist, to **naakaN-**
extremely **getaaN**
eye **buiH (-ha)**
eyebrow **ga'imbehe (ga'imbehi)**
eyelash(es) **budusii' (-a)**

face goob<u>ai</u> (goob<u>ai</u>)
fall (autumn) yebaa'ni
fall, last munnagwa yebaa'ni
fall, next egi yebaa'ni gimaginde
fall, this egi yebaa'ni
farm, to dewaseange-
fart bishupe (-ha)
fat yuhu; yuhupe (-ha)
father ape' (-a)
father's brother (older) bia'ape' (-a)
father's brother (younger) dei'ape' (-a)
father's cousin (female) baha' (-a)
father's sister baha' (-a)
favorite food tsaa-dekape (-ha)
feces gwidape (-ha)
feel, to deesu'a-; suaN-; wesunga-
feel good about, to tsaawesunga-
female cousin, older bazi' (-a)
female cousin, younger nammi' (-a)
female friend dei' (-a)
fifty manegiseemote
fifty cents u sengw<u>ai</u>bi ma'<u>ai</u>
find, to da'oda-
fire gotoope (-ha); wahyande (wahyandi)
fire, to make gotoo-
first ha['] yangenaa'
first thing ha['] yangenaa'
fish b<u>ai</u>ngwi (b<u>ai</u>ngwi)
five manegite (manegiti)
five of (something) manegitee' (manegitei')
fix (with the hands), to mabizhiaN-
flatulence bishupe (-ha)
flesh duku (duki)
flicker, northern wobindotadegi' (-a)
flowing ogw<u>ai</u>deN
fly, to yeze-
fly away (from the speaker), to yezegwaH-/yezekuaH-
foggy, to be baagenaiH-
food dekape (-ha)
food, favorite tsaa-dekape (-ha)
footprint nanambuipe (-ha)

forehead **ga'i (ga'i)**
Fort Hall **Botoode**
four **watsewite (watsewiti)**
four, only **watsewiteese**
fox **waahni' (-a)**
freezing (cold), to be **de'ase-**
friend (female) **dei' (-a)**
friend (male) **daga' (-a); hainji (-ha)**
from **nai'; naite**
from where **haganai'; haganaite**
front, in **wenangwa; wenangwaku**
frozen **nade'asengepe (-ha)**
fry bread **yuhudegumahannipe (-ha)**
frying pan **degwasenge' (-a)**

gas, intestinal **bishupe (-ha)**
get dressed, to **nawasoaH-**
get hot, to **gutseniH-**
get to be (in time), to **naakiH-**
get up, to **yeze-**
ghost **tso'ape (-ha)**
Gibson District (Fort Hall Reservation) **Bohogoi'**
girl friend **dehainji (-ha)**
give, to **utu"-**
give (by hand), to **tsa'utu"-**
go, to **mi'a-**
go and [+ verb] **-kua'**
go and [+ verb] and return **-nei-**
go and come back, to **gooni-**
go back, to **go'aiH-**
go in, to **ya'iH-**
go out, to **do'aiH-; mi'awa'iH-**
go to bed, to **ha[']bi-**
good **tsaaN**
good afternoon **tsaangu yeitabai'yi; tsaangu yeitatabai'yi**
good evening **tsaangu yeyeika**
good morning **tsaangu beaichehku; tsaangu baiche**
grandchild(ren) (by one's daughter) [female speech] **gagu'(-a)**
grandchild(ren) (by one's daughter) [male speech] **dogo' (-a)**
grandchild(ren) (by one's son) [female speech] **hutsi' (-a)**
grandchild(ren) (by one's son) [male speech] **genu' (-a)**

grandfather (maternal) **dogo' (-a)**
grandfather (paternal) **genu' (-a)**
grandmother (maternal) **gagu' (-a)**
grandmother (paternal) **hutsi' (-a)**
grass (green) **buhipe (-ha)**
green **buhibite (buhibiti)**
green, to grow **buhihsea-**
grey **aishimbite (aishimbiti)**
ground **sogo, sogope (-ha)**
grow, to **sea"-; seakaN-**
grow green, to **buhihsea-**

habitually [+ verb] **-kwai'nna**
half (in reference to money) **sengwaibiN; u sengwaibiN**
hair (head) **bambipe (-ha); bambi (bambi)**
hand **mo' (-a)**
hand, by/with the **tsa-**
hang, to **nazawaiyiH-**
happen, to **naa-; naha-**
happen to see, to **bu[']ni-**
hard **getande (getandi)**
hat **dezo[']woi (-ha)**
have, to **ba'i; gande, gandehwe, gandee'**
have to, to **dugu**
head **bambi (bambi)**
head of lettuce **buhi-dekape (-ha)**
hear, to **nangaH-; denangaH-; denangahka-**
hear well, to **tsaan denangaH-**
heard, to be **nanangaH-**
heart **bihiN (bihiN)**
heat up, to **gutseniH-**
her **u**
here (not close enough to touch) **aiki; saiki**
here, over **saitu**
here, right **iki; siki; sikiteN**
here it is **iki ma'i**
hide, to **wazi-; wazika-**
high over **ba'ande**
him **u**
Hispanic **doyadaiboo' (-a)**
hit, to **wepa'i-**

holes, to cause many dedotadawengeN-
horse bungu (bungui/bungi)
hot, to be ede'iN-
hospital natesu'ungahni (natesu'ungahni)
hot (of weather), to be continuously gutsenihka'ai-
hot, to get gutseniH-
house gahniN (gahniN)
how haganni; hagannihatu; hagai'; hagaiti
how come? haganni'yunde?
how many himbaigandee' (himbaigandei')
how much himbaigaN; himbaigande
how much (money), for himbaigandengahtu
hundred biaseemote (biaseemoti)
hungry, to be very bahodeyai-
husband nadainape' (-a)
husband, sister's [female speech] nadainape' (-a)

I ne
Idaho Falls (Idaho) Dembimbosaage
in duN; gaH; -gati; gupa; gupángu
in addition to -ma'ai; -ma'aiku
in front of wenangwa; wenangwaku
in there sa['}bai; su['}bai'
Indian ne['}we (ne['}wi)
Indian, Bannock bannaite' (-a)
Indian, Blackfoot baki'eheÕ (-a)
Indian, Crow a'aa' (-a)
Indian, Kiowa yamba'i (-ha)
Indian, Nez Perce newezoika'i (-ha)
Indian, Shoshoni ne['}we (ne['}wi); sosoni' (-a)
Indian, Southern Plains yamba'i (-ha)
Indian corn ha['}niibe (-ha)
Indian language newedaigwape (-ha)
Indian language, in the ne['}we duN
Indian language, speaking the daan newedaigwa'nna
Indian potatoes basigoo' (-a)
intestinal gas bishupe (-ha)
intestines go'hai (go'hai)
it u; ma
it is said mai

jackrabbit ga['] mmu (-i)
John Dzoon (-ha)
journalist deboogwapi (-ha)
judge denihanigwapi (-ha)
judge, to denihani-
juniper tree, Utah waapi (-ta)
just (adv) da'ga

kid, nice little tsaandetsi' (-a)
kidney dagipoo' (-a)
Kiowa Indian yamba'i (-ha)
knead (dough), to domahanni'-

land sogo, sogope (-ha)
language daigwape (-ha)
last fall munna'gwa yeba'ni
last spring munna'gwa dahwani
last summer munna'gwa da'za
last winter munna'gwa dommo
last year munna'gwa
late gaiyu'uN
later binna['] gwa; binnagwaseN
lawyer denihanigwapi (-ha)
learn by listening, to denangabizhiaN-
left (to do something) and came back -nei'
left over, to be biiyaiH-
lettuce, head of buhidekape (-ha)
lie, to ha['] bi-
light, electric degupita' (-a)
like -niku; wa'i; -ni
like, to tsaasuaN-; tsaawesunga-
like (by tasting), to gesunga-
like the taste of, to tsaangesunga-
little deinde (deindi)
little (bit), a deigu' (-a); deingu' (-a)
live, to naakaN-
located, to be hannihkaN-
long gebedande (gebedandi)
long ago beaiN; beaim beeN
long time ago, a beaiN; beaim beeN
look (like), to nabuiH-

look like (something), to **wa'i nabuiH-**
lot, a **sooN; sooseN**
loud, to be/sound **bia-nanangande**
lunch, to eat **dab<u>ai</u>dekaH-**
lung(s) **sowoN (-na)**

maize **ha[']niibe (-ha)**
make, to **naha-; naa-**
make a round trip, to **gooni-**
male cousin **ada' (-a)**
male cousin, younger **dawi' (-a)**
male friend **daga' (-a); hainji (-ha)**
man, old **tsugupe' (-a)**
man, young **duibichi' (-a)**
many **sooN; soonde, soondehwe, soondee'**
mark a circle, to **gooni-**
maternal grandfather **dogo' (-a)**
maternal grandmother **gagu' (-a)**
maybe **gia'; giasé['] ba; se['] ba; sebagia'**
me **ne<u>ai</u>**
meat **duku (duki)**
meat, deer **deheya'an duku (duki)**
meat, turkey **guyungwi'yaa'an duku (duki)**
medicine **natesu'uN (natesu'una)**
merchant **nadewagagwapi (-ha)**
mess up, to **su'ah<u>ai</u>bei-**
Mexican (person) **doyadaiboo' (-a)**
Mexican-American (person) **doyadaiboo' (-a)**
midnight **dogw<u>ai</u>-duga['] ni**
might (VERB) **wizha**
milk **bizhi' (-a)**
milk cow (female) **bizhi'guchuN (bizhi'guchuna)**
mine **ne; neaN**
morning, early **be<u>ai</u>chehku**
morning, in the (early) **be<u>ai</u>chehkuseN**
morning, this **egi be<u>ai</u>chehku**
morning, tomorrow **iwaa' be<u>ai</u>chehku**
morning, yesterday **gendum be<u>ai</u>chehku**
mother **bia' (-a)**
mother's brother **ada' (-a)**
mother's sister **bia' (-a)**

mountain sheep **duku (duki)**
mountain trout **tsaa-baingwi (tsaa-baingwi)**
much **sooN; sooseN; soonde, soondehwe, soondei'**
music **hubia' (-a)**
must [verb] **dugu**
my **ne; neaN**

name **naniha (nanihai)**
nasal mucus **mubishipe (-ha)**
neck **do'yoN (-na)**
necklace **godokoN (-na)**
need, to **suaN-; suwai-**
new **ege-; egebichi (-ha)**
next fall **egi yeba'ni gimaginde**
next spring **egi dahwani gimaginde**
next summer **egi da'zan gimaginde**
next to **gewaga; gewagahku; baihyugi**
next winter **egi dommo gimaginde**
Nez Perce (Indian) **newezoiga'i (-ha)**
night **duga'ni**
noon **dabai'yi; dogwai-dabail'lyi**
no **gai'**
northern flicker **wobindotadegi' (-a)**
nostrils **muubindadawennaN (-na)**
not **gai**
not good **gizhaa**
not know, to **gai sumbana'i-**
not like (taste), to **deche gesunga-**
not much **gai himbaigaN; gai himbaigande**
not there, it's **gaiháiwa'i**
not yet **gaisheN; gaisheseN**
nothing there, there's **gaiháiwa'i**
now **egi**

obey, to **denangabizhiaN-**
okay **maiku**
old **beaitembe (-ha)**
older brother **babi' (-a)**
older cousin (female) **bazi' (-a)**
older sister **bazi' (-a)**
on **maN**

on top of ba'aN; ba'angu
one semme' (-a); sewe; daa
one's daaN
oneself benneN, bennaN
onion genga (geng<u>ai</u>)
only da'ga; -teese
operate (something) by hand, to dezahani-
otherwise noondea
our dahaN, dammeN
outside maitenga; maitengaku; maitengate
oven-baked bread degumahanipe (-ha)
over ba'ande
over here s<u>ai</u>tu
over that way soto
over there aku; saku
owl mumbichi (-ha)
own, its beN

package nadatewade (nadatewadi)
pants gusa (gus<u>ai</u>)
paternal grandfather genu' (-a)
paternal grandmother hutsi' (-a)
perfume, skunk's bishupe (-ha)
people at (a specific location) gahtei'
people say m<u>ai</u>
perhaps gia'; giasé['[]ba; se['[]ba; sebagia'
person ne['[]we (ne['[]wi)
pick up with the hands, to hiwange-
pine tree wongo['[]bi (-ta)
pink <u>ai</u>nga'<u>ai</u>bi' (-ti/-ta)
plan, to nasundeganaaH-
plant, to maseange-
plate a['[]wo (awoi')
point to/at, to tsitsugaH-
policeman dedakooni' (-a)
pot witua' (witu<u>ai</u>')
potato tsiinna' (-a)
purple <u>ai</u>kwehibite (<u>ai</u>kwehibiti)
put, to -tegi-
put (something) by hand, to tsategi-
put on socks, to dap<u>ai</u>hyaaH-

quarter (twenty-five cents) **dubiichi (-ha)**

railroad **gunawaimungu (gunawaimungi)**
rain, to **wei-**
rain hard, to **baa'ema-**
rain lightly, to **baazagaiH-**
rain periodically, to **wei'i-**
raise (animals), to **maseange-**
reading materials (in English) **daan daiboo' ded<u>ai</u>gwa'nna**
read, to **ded<u>ai</u>gwa-**
really **getaaN**
red **<u>ai</u>nga-; <u>ai</u>ngabite (<u>ai</u>ngabiti); <u>ai'ai</u>ngabitehwe (-tehi)**
restaurant **deka-gahni (deka-gahni)**
restroom **nado'<u>ai</u>gahni (nado'<u>ai</u>gahni); neweguchu (-na); biaguchu (-na)**
return, to **go'<u>ai</u>H-**
rib(s) **a[']waN (-na)**
rib cage **a[']waN (-na)**
right at **dogw<u>ai</u>**
right here **iki; siki; sikiteN**
river **ogw<u>ai</u>deN**
run, to **nuki-**
run (of motor), to **guhn<u>ai</u>ki-**
run fast (with random movement), to **nukigwai'i-**

salad **buhi-dekape (-ha)**
salmon **agai' (agai')**
say, to **niikwi-**
secretary **deboogwapi (-ha)**
see, to **bui-**
see by chance, to **bu[']ni-**
self **benneN, bennaN**
sell, to **nadewaga-**
set, to (of sun) **ya'ihwa-**
set (something) down, to **dahna-**
sew, to **dezakeena-**
sheep **sii-bungu (sii-bungi)**
shirt **gwasu'uN (gwasu'una)**
shit **gwidape (-ha)**
shoe **nambe (nambeha/nampeha)**
should **wizha**

shoulder(s) **tsoape (-ha)**
Shoshoni (Indian) **ne[']we (ne[']wi); sosoni' (-a)**
Shoshoni (language) **sosoni'daigwape (-ha); newedaigwape (-ha)**
Shoshoni (language), in **ne[']we duN**
shy, to be **nade'eyan nasu'waiN-**
sing, to **denito'ai-**
singer **denito'aigwapi (-ha)**
sister, younger **nammi' (-a)**
sister-in-law [female speech] **bahambia' (-a)**
sister's husband [female speech] **nadainape' (-a)**
sister's husband [male speech] **dai'zhi (dai'zhi)**
sister's son [male speech] **ada' (-a)**
sit, to **gade-**
situated, to be **hannihkaN-**
six **naafaite (naafaiti)**
six (of something) **naafaitee' (naafaitei')**
six o'clock, at **naafaitenga daa naakihka**
skirt **gwasu'uN (gwasu'una)**
skunk **buhni'atsi (-ha)** (also **bohni'atsi**)
small **deinde (deindi)**
smell, to **gwanaa"-**
smoky, to be **gwiipusiaH-**
snot **mubishipe (-ha)**
snow **dakabi (-ta)**
snow, to **dakaweiH-**
snow a lot, to **dakadua'ai-**
sock(s) **dapaihyaa' (-a)**
socks, to put on **dapaihyaaH-**
soft **yu'nainde (yu'naindi), yu'naindehwe (yu'naindehi), yu'naindee'
 (yu'naindei')**
somebody **daa**
someone **daa**
someone's **daaN**
something **daa**
sometimes **sesewe'**
son **dua' (-a)**
song **hubia' (-a)**
Southern Plains Indian **yamba'i (-ha)**
sow, to **maseange-**
speak, to **daigwa-**
speaking (the) Indian (language) **daan newedaigwa'nna**

speech d<u>a</u>igwape (-ha)
spine gwah<u>a</u>intsuhni (gwah<u>a</u>intsuhni)
split, to wepagu'i-
spring (time) dahwaa[']ni
spring, last munnagwa dahwaani
spring, next egi dahwaani gimaginde
spring, this egi dahwaani
sprinkle, to baazagaiH-
sprout (of plants), to buhihsea-
stand, to we[']ne-
start (to), to -tegi-/-degi-
starving, to be bahodeyai-
stew saape (-ha)
stomach sape (-ha)
store nadewengahni (nadewengahni)
stove gotoonoo' (-a)
stream ogw<u>a</u>ideN
study, to debofoi-
summer (time) da[']zaN
summer, last munnagwa da'za
summer, next egi da'zan gimaginde
summer, this egi da'za
sun dab<u>ai</u>
sunny, to be dab<u>ai</u>shu'aiH-
sunshine, to have dab<u>ai</u>shu'ai-gande
sweetheart dehimbe (-ha)
swim, to bahaabi-

talk, to d<u>a</u>igwa-
teach, to dezateboofoingeH-; tsateboofoiN-; tsateboofoingeH-
tell, to niikwi-
ten seemote (seemoti)
testicle noo'yo (noo'yi)
thank you <u>a</u>isheN
that adeN; aka; akaN; aseN; ma; made; madeN; maka; makaN;
    maseN; odeN; oka; okaN; oseN; sadeN; saka; sakaN; sodeN; soka;
    sokaN; sudeN; suka; sukaN; udeN; uka; ukaN; useN
that's because ade'uka
that's why sunni'yunde
their adeeN; adeheN; <u>a</u>ideheN; ideeN
there oku

them adehi; madehi; madei'; odei'; odehi; sadehi; sadei'; saidehi;
    saidei; sidei'; sidehi; sodehi; sodei'; sudehi; sudei'; udehi; udei'
then binna[']gwa; demaseN; subai'; wihyu
there soku; suku; uku; ukuhti
these aidee'; aidehi; aidehwe; aidei'; idee'; idei'; ideheN; idehi;
    idehwe; madeheN; madehwe; saidee'; saideeN; saideheN;
    saidehwe; sidee'; sideeN;,sideheN; sidehwe
they adee'; adehwe; aidee'; aidehi'; aidei'
they say mai
think, to suaN-
think well of, to tsaasuaN-
this aideN; aika; aikaN; ideN; ika; ikaN; isheN; ma; made; madeN;
    maka; makaN; maseN; saideN; saika; saikaN; sideN; sika; sikaN
this afternoon egi yeitabai'yi
this evening egi yeika
this fall egi yeba'ni
this morning egi beaichehku
this spring egi dahwani
this summer egi da'za
this winter egi do[']mmo
those adee'; adehi; adehwe; madeheN; madehwe; odee'; odeeN;
    odeheN; odehwe; sadee'; sadeeN; sadeheN' sadehwe; sodee';
    sodeeN; sodeheN; sodehwe; sudee'; sudeeN; sudeheN; sudehwe;
    udee'; udeeN; udehwe
through gaba
to -baidu; gahtu
to where hagapundu
today egi dabai'yi
toe(s) daseweeki' (-a)
toilet nado'aigahni (nado'aigahni); gwida-gahni (gwida-gahni)
tomato tsiambe (-ha)
tomorrow iwaa'
tomorrow afternoon iwaa' yeitabai'yi
tomorrow morning iwaa' beaichehku
tomorrow evening iwaa' yeika
tomorrow night iwaa' duga'ni
too deaseN
toward -baidu
train gunawaimungu (gunawaimungi)
tree soho[']bi (-ta)
trot, to boyokami'a-

trout, mountain tsaa-baingwi (tsaa-baingwi)
turkey guyungwi'yaa' (-a)
turkey meat guyungwi'yaa'an duku (duki)
two wahatehwe (wahatehi)
two hundred wahambiaseemote (wahambiaseemoti)

udder (of cow) bizhi' (-a)
uncle dei'ape' (-a)
under dukaN; dukangu; dukai
understand (by hearing), to nangasumbaaduH-
unpleasant(ly) deche
us nemmi
usually su'ana
used to noha
Utah juniper tree waapi (-ta)
Ute Indian yuuta' (-a)

vendor nadewagagwapi (-ha)
venison deheya'an duku (duki)
very getaaN

walk (of men) [male speech] boyokami'a-
want, to suaN-; suwai-
want to [+ verb], to -suaN-
wash, to gozho[']hai-
wash dishes, to awogazho[']hai-
watch (timepiece) [noun] dabai
watch, to dembuiH-
water baa' (bai')
we dahwe; damme; nehwe; nemme
weasel babizhii' (-a)
what hagai'; hagaiti; hagani; haganihatu; hi[']nni (hi[']nna)
what time (of day)? hinga dabai
what way?, in hagani; haganihatu
when -gu; himbai
where haga'; haga'aku; haga'a[']nna
where at haga'ahti
where from haganai'; haganaite
where to hagapundu
which hagadeN
while -gu
white dosa-; dosabite (-biti), dosabi

white person **daiboo' (-a)**
who **hagadeN**
why **haganni'yunde**
wife **gwee' (-a); gwehe (gwehi); nawa'aipe' (-a)**
wife, brother's [female speech] **bahambia' (-a)**
wild carrots **yamba (yambai)**
will be **du'i**
window **banabui' (-a)/banabuiH (-ha)**
windy, to be **neai-**
wing **gasa (gasai)**
winter (time) **do[']mmo**
winter, last **munnagwa dommo**
winter, next **egi dommo gimaginde**
winter, this **egi do[']mmo**
with **ma'aiH; ma'aihku**
with (instrument) **maN**
within **gupa; gupángu**
wood **gu[']na (gu[']na)**
word **daigwape (-ha)**
work, to **dede'ai-**
work for, to **dede'ainge-**
write, to **deboo-**
writer **deboogwapi (-ha)**
written materials in English **daan daiboo' dedaigwa'nna**

yampa root **yamba (yambai)**
year **do[']mmo**
year, last **munna[']gwa**
yellow **ohapite (ohapiti)**
yes **haa'**
yesterday **genduN**
yesterday afternoon **gendu yeitabai'yi**
yesterday evening **gendu yeika**
yesterday morning **gendum beaichehku**
yet, not **gaisheN; gaisheseN**
you **e[']mmi; eN; e[']nne; mehwe; memme**
your **eN; meheN; memmeN**
young man **duibichi' (a)**
younger brother **dawi' (a)**
younger cousin (male) **dawi' (-a)**
younger sister **nammi' (-a)**

Index